all
or nothing

JESSE SCHENKER

all
or nothing

ONE CHEF'S APPETITE FOR THE EXTREME

DEY ST.
AN IMPRINT OF WILLIAM MORROW PUBLISHERS

DEY ST.

HarperCollins books may be purchased for educational, business, or sales promotional use. For information please e-mail the Special Markets Department at SPsales@harpercollins.com.

FIRST EDITION

Designed by Paula Russell Szafranski
Title-page art © by Jaimie Duplass/Shutterstock, Inc.

Library of Congress Cataloging-in-Publication Data has been applied for.

ISBN 978-0-06-233930-0

14 15 16 17 18   OV/RRD   10 9 8 7 6 5 4 3 2 1

To my warrior wife:

You're the only one who ever truly understands me, and

your capacity for love is amazing.

How you continuously manage all that you do with such

strength and beauty is remarkable.

Thank you for our two beautiful children and for

continuing to love me and stand by me as we build our

life together. I am nothing without you.

"I love you more than blood."

To my mom and dad:

Today I see and feel what you've known for as long as

I have been breathing air.

The love for a child—your love for your children—is so strong

it hurts. You two are amazing in ways I never understood before

becoming a parent, too. It was always there; I was just too

self-absorbed to see it. Now that I feel that same love for my

own children, I'm able to fully appreciate and respect

everything you've done for me and continue to do every day.

I love you.

♥

Contents

Contents

Mise en Place

Mise en place: A French phrase ("putting in place") used in professional kitchens to refer to the organizing and arranging of ingredients that a cook will require during his or her shift.

What plate does the fried geoduck go on?" I quizzed my sous chef Ed.

"The small square," he said, referring to the traditional Japanese plates I'd purchased the week before.

"Right. And what comes next?"

"Black bass, wood tea, sardine, chawanmushi," Audrey rattled off. Good. As a sous chef, she'd be up at the pass helping me plate, so she had to know the exact order the dishes should be served in by heart. It wasn't easy keeping track of twenty-seven courses—and those were just the savory ones. I glanced around and caught a few frustrated looks passing between the five people on my team. They were tired and cold. We'd been up almost all night getting the elaborate meal ready, and the March evening air still held a gust of winter. But we always sat outside to go over every detail before diving into a completely unknown menu for the first time, and by now I was superstitious.

1

Most New York City kitchen staffs debut a new menu once each season after months of preparation, but we did it every month with only a week or two to get ready. I knew I was asking a lot, perhaps too much. And this menu, featuring dozens of courses of traditional Japanese ingredients made with French techniques and my own whimsical flair, would be the most difficult to execute yet.

As we sat there going over everything my legs started twitching and my feet started tapping. I couldn't sit still. Without thinking, I jumped up and paced around the small outdoor area. "Remember, it's not just about the food—it has to be an experience," I lectured. "I want theatrics. Everything has to be timed perfectly, the execution spot-on."

"Yes, Chef," my cooks said in unison, and then we headed inside to start preparing the meal.

It was only two weeks before that I had taken my wife Lindsay to dinner at Soto on Sixth Avenue and been blown away by the simple yet ingeniously creative dishes, like the Sliced Live Sea Clam Marinated in Truffle Ginger Soy Sauce; Daikon Pickle with Shiso, Bonito Flake, Ginger Shoots, and Pickled Squash; and uni, one of my favorite ingredients, made a dozen different ways, with black soybean milk skin, in a simple soy reduction and wasabi, and in endless sushi and maki roll varieties.

When we got home that night, Lindsay went to check on our one-year-old son Eddie while I jumped on the computer to read every Japanese food blog I could find. After Lindsay went to bed, I walked over to my collection of more than 300 cookbooks and pulled down *Nobu: The Cookbook* by Nobuyuki Matsuhisa and *Morimoto: The New Art of Japa-*

nese Cooking by Masaharu Morimoto, then pored over them until the sun came up. By then I had written out the shell of a ten-course tasting menu that I quickly emailed to Christina Han with a note. "Let's do a Japanese tasting menu for the next Monday with Jesse."

Eddie was awake by then, and I heard Lindsay begin to stir in the next room. Part of me wanted to stay and spend time with them, to see Eddie for the first time in over twenty-four hours and help Lindsay with his morning routine, but a greater force compelled me to grab my keys and leave the apartment. I had to get to Recette.

A few months after Recette had opened, I'd started to feel bogged down by the monotony of cooking the same food day after day, handling the exact same ingredients and meticulously preparing identical plates one after the other. Every time I went out to dinner I was inspired by something I ate, but I knew that it wouldn't work to change Recette's menu too often. Inspired by Tom Colicchio's "Tom Tuesdays," I came up with the idea of "Mondays with Jesse." Once a month I closed down the restaurant and let my imagination run free, coming up with an elaborate tasting menu that allowed me to flex my culinary muscles. I would never put ingredients that I wasn't intimately familiar with, like the traditional Japanese ones, on the regular menu, but Mondays with Jesse gave me license to experiment with new flavors, combinations, and even entire cuisines. Before long, roughly the same group of foodies started coming to these dinners and became my lab rats, allowing me to do in the kitchen what I had always loved most—play.

These tasting menus always consisted of ten courses, but

as soon as I started experimenting with the Japanese menu my imagination ran wilder than ever before. If we served a raw prawn for one course, we could fry the shrimp head and serve it as another. When presenting the raw geoduck clam, why not follow it with a piece of fried geoduck belly? Every time we thought we had the menu finalized I kept adding more courses—for instance, a play on shrimp toast that we called Salt and Pepper Chicharron; a takeoff on shabu-shabu, with broth that was flavored with fish bones and topped with raw beef; or a spin on bagels and lox that used a crispy bagel chip, whipped tofu instead of cream cheese, and raw Hamachi in place of the salmon.

Even as my staff asked, "Are you crazy? Why are we doing so many courses?" I kept pushing further. Simply cooking twenty-seven courses wasn't enough for me. I found new ways to make the entire experience more extreme by buying elaborate chopsticks, researching traditional Japanese vessels and cookware, and coming up with yet more dishes to serve.

We had only two weeks to develop each of the recipes from scratch. I wanted to make a chawanmushi, a traditional egg custard that normally consists of dashi and egg and has the consistency of a light crème brûlée. My idea was to include lobster, so I played around with making lobster truffles by pureeing lobster meat with lobster roe, forming balls out of the puree using plastic wrap, and then steaming them, but they came out too rubbery. Finally, we folded the lobster puree in with the eggs, which turned them bright red, and then served the chawanmushi with raw diced lobster meat tossed with sesame and cilantro on top. The color was striking, and it tasted like an explosion of lobster and egg.

Another dish I was determined to make was a traditional rice ball, or Donburi, but I didn't know how. First I tried cooking white rice and frying it just to see what happened. It was okay, but needed refining. Next I tried overcooking the rice and then laying it out on a sheet pan. I put it in the freezer to set and then cut it into squares and pan-fried them. The outside got nice and crispy, but the inside didn't stay together. I did round after round, often in the middle of the night after Recette was done with service and everyone else had gone home. Finally, we made a rice porridge, drained it, and reserved the liquid, which was starchy and tasted like rice. Once the rice had cooled, we added gelatin and cut the rice into squares that we breaded and fried. The inside was still liquid and burst in your mouth when you took a bite. Delicious. We served it with pork belly and mushroom as the final savory course of the meal.

As we went back into Recette's tiny kitchen after our meeting outside I could sense that everyone was on edge. On some level I knew that I was making them nervous as I laid out dozens of tiny note cards listing every table and course so we could keep track of each course and cross it off whenever a plate was served. But I couldn't rein it in. I continued hollering the same instructions they'd heard several times by then as I tore through the kitchen, checking everything for the hundredth time. I moved a thin slice of raw fish a millimeter to the left on the hot rock that seared it, I tightened the kelp envelope surrounding the sliced mackerel so the diners' senses would be overwhelmed by the smell and taste of the sea when opening it, and I checked the yakitori grills heating in the oven. "The grills aren't hot enough,"

I called to Christina as I continued moving through the kitchen.

I stopped in front of the burner where the consommé for the shabu-shabu was simmering. My mind was spinning with too many thoughts at once. I had to check in with Christina Lee about the five dessert courses she was in charge of and then get to the front of the house to look at the reservations list and psych up the hostess and waitstaff to execute a great service. My hand shook slightly as I pulled the tasting spoon from the back pocket of my jeans, a simple movement burned so clearly into my muscle memory that for the briefest of moments I forgot where I was.

There had been a spoon in my back pocket for as long as I could remember, but the spoon's intended use had changed so completely that even I was caught off guard at times. Once I had carried a spoon to cook drugs on the streets of Florida, and now it was there to prepare haute cuisine for Manhattan's foodie elite. This was a transformation I could not have imagined taking place over a span of eight years. But as I snapped to my senses and dipped the spoon into the dank-ass broth the truth hit me that I was just as addicted as ever—it was only the substance that had changed.

CHAPTER ONE

Braise

Braise: A combination cooking method using both moist and dry heat. First the food is seared at a high temperature, and then it is finished by simmering in a covered pot with a variable amount of liquid, resulting in a particular flavor.

The story my mom always tells about me when I was a kid goes like this: By the time I was a year old, I was already climbing out of my crib. My older sister Joee (pronounced *Joey*) never climbed out. She was happy to stay in that crib until my parents decided that she was old enough for a bed. But I wouldn't stay put. I climbed out over and over again until my parents finally realized they couldn't keep me contained any longer. They got me a toddler bed, but of course I wouldn't stay in it either. I wouldn't even stay in my room.

The townhouse we lived in back then in Tamarac, Florida, had a steep flight of stairs right outside my door. My parents were scared that I would fall down the stairs when I came barreling out, so eventually they were forced to place a latch on the outside of the door and lock me into my room at night. When my mother came in to get me in the morning, she says, she found me perched on a nightstand that I had pushed into the corner and reaching up with my small pudgy arm to rip more wallpaper off the wall. Strip by strip, I'd torn it down all the way from the ceiling to the floor in clean, straight lines.

I don't remember doing that, but I certainly believe it. I can feel in my bones exactly what it must have been like for me as a baby, locked in that room but full of restless energy and the urgent need to escape. For as long as I can remember, I've had this unquenchable thirst to keep moving, going, and doing. I've never felt comfortable in my own skin and have always needed an outlet for that uneasiness. When I was a kid, my leg was always twitching, my foot constantly tapping. I just couldn't sit still. "Jesse has a lot of energy," my mother would say apologetically when I knocked over yet another plant or vase, destroying the perfect order of our home.

But order was hard to come by in those days, and not just because of my own odd behavior. Our family moved a couple of times within just a few years, finally landing in a wealthy gated community called Cypress Head within the city of Parkland, Florida. Cypress Head was a giant cul-de-sac, a three-mile-long circle where you couldn't go forward, only right or left. No matter which way you turned, you just kept going around that huge circle. Suddenly we were in a big house surrounded by golf courses and even a nature preserve. It was heaven to my parents, especially my dad, who'd grown up in a Brooklyn tenement, but I always felt like an outsider. My dad's mantra was, "Play the part, act like you belong," but I couldn't even pretend to fit in there. Parkland had no culture or real community. Everyone had come there from somewhere else, and the city had nothing that could anchor its residents. That left me feeling bored and lonely, even when I wasn't alone.

I responded by concocting imaginary friends, a whole Rolodex of characters I called upon. Late at night I'd lie in bed talking to "Blake," rehashing my day and planning some sort of shenanigans for the morning. Joee would yell at me from the next room, "Shut up, Jesse, there's no one there!" but I never listened to her.

From the outside it must have looked like I had a picture-perfect childhood. My dad worked hard and provided more than enough for our family, while my mom stayed home with Joee and me and put all of her heart and soul into raising us kids. We went on family vacations every year, my dad coached every single one of my sports teams, and Joee and I literally had everything we could ask for, to the extent that we never even had to ask.

From the time I was a toddler I admired my dad's work ethic. He started a dental supply business out of the trunk of his car when he first moved to Florida in the late '70s and sold it to a Fortune 500 company thirty years later. When I was a kid, he also had side gigs and was always out hustling, looking to make a few extra bucks.

Despite working long hours, my dad found a way to spend a lot of time with Joee and me. But sometimes even when he was with me it seemed like he wasn't all there. He was often distracted by his own worries and anxieties. I didn't know at the time that he was drinking a lot and partying. When I was five years old, my mom threatened to leave my dad if he didn't stop. The next thing I knew there was no alcohol in the house, not even wine on Passover. My mom completely stopped drinking too, as a show of support, until they were able to reintroduce alcohol years later in a more moderate way. But alcohol or no alcohol, they were always going five rounds about something. Money was the big topic now. My dad made it, but never enough; my mother spent it, but always too much.

Compulsiveness became my lifeline. It helped me escape. When you're a lonely, frustrated kid, there's nothing like the painless pleasure of living in distraction. Constructing tree forts, climbing on the roof, kicking holes in the walls, and hammering screwdrivers into tree trunks were some of my favorite ways to pass the time. I needed a physical release for all my energy. I could never just *be*. But I was never satisfied, and the more I acted out the more unsettled I grew.

The discomfort I felt in my own skin got worse until eventually it seemed like my body was rebelling against me. I remember waking up almost every night with agonizing growing pains. My mom would lie in my tiny bed with me, sometimes for hours at a time. She made up a magician named Shandoo and told me stories about him as she rubbed my legs until I fell asleep.

Food was my first real escape from the unease within me. When I couldn't focus on anything for more than a few minutes at a time, food caught my attention like nothing else. Food meant very little in our house. My mom took care of feeding us kids and she did her best to cook for us, but she was no chef. For a typical dinner she'd boil penne pasta, put it in a bowl with mozzarella cheese, and melt it in the microwave. On other nights she put ground meat in taco shells or made a Tyson chicken.

Our kitchen lay mostly dormant until my great-grandma, Nana Mae, came over and brought it to life. On holidays and special occasions she took over the kitchen and it then became my refuge. Watching her at the stove, dressed impeccably with an apron on over her clothes, I could sense that cooking meant more to her than just making food. The way she talked about, touched, and experienced food reminded me of the way a gardener cultivates flowers or a tailor attends to the details of a hand-stitched suit. There was a purpose to Nana Mae's cooking. She was doing it with love, expressing herself through the dishes she made. As I watched her lovingly wield a paring knife like a samurai brandishing his sword just to cut something simple like apple wedges, I was fucking mesmerized. My leg suddenly stopped twitching, and I sat at the Formica table in awe and homed in on one new desire: to create something of my own in the kitchen.

From that moment forward I would have moved heaven and earth to get in a kitchen—any kitchen. When I was four years old, I started making up excuses to go to Nana Mae's house just so I could watch her cook. Once there, I stirred the pot, tasted for seasoning, fetched ingredients, did the prep work, and then had a snack or two until it was time to eat. Nana Mae taught me the foundation of cooking. Watching her, I figured out how to prep, slice, dice, season, and build flavors to make a delicious meal. Nana Mae's kitchen was a vivid, intense world of new and exciting smells and flavors. To this day the slightest hint of onion reminds me of those beautiful hours I spent in her kitchen, learning as I watched her work.

Once Nana Mae saw my eagerness to create, she just stood back and didn't meddle. She was the perfect person to nurture my passion because she left me to my own devices. She never said, "Do this," or "Do that."

For me, being in the kitchen was like taking a Xanax. I finally had an outlet for all of the emotions that were too uncomfortable for me to really feel. I had never known what to do with those feelings. In the kitchen I had a sense of freedom and space and, most important, order and clarity. It was the only time the restlessness within me subsided.

My early experiments didn't always turn out well. In fact, most of them were fucking awful. But I didn't care so much about the results; I just wanted to play with food. The sound of an egg cracking was intriguing; the empty shell was a mystery. I went on a recon mission to learn everything I could about food, especially what combinations tasted good together and what didn't. I never stopped experimenting. When my family went out for dinner, it was always to the same Chinese place. I put the fried noodles in a bowl with the hot mustard, sweet and sour, and soy sauce and mixed it all together. I called it "kakaballee." It tasted gross, but I didn't care. I had created something. At home I took ground beef, which my mom called "chop meat," and wrapped it around hot dogs to make a sort of corn dog, but with the beef on the outside. Then I cloaked it in bacon and baked it in the oven. It was disgusting. But I loved the look of it and the experience of building layer upon layer of texture and flavor.

Nana Mae died when I was eight years old, and though I was too young to really understand why, her death inspired me to start cooking even more. My mom noticed this and started asking me to help her make dinner. She laminated a place mat so I could use it to chop vegetables with a small knife and even prepare meals. When other kids were outside playing, I was in the kitchen, helping my mom make dinner or elaborately fanning apple slices around a plate before I ate them.

Most of my happy childhood memories took place in the kitchen. My dad almost never cooked, but the two things he could make were French fries and pancakes. His homemade French fry days were the best. Joee and I would wake up to the smell of oil and run into the kitchen yelling, "Daddy's cooking!" My dad would hand me my place mat, a potato, and a peeler, and I'd sit at the breakfast bar, peeling the potato inward toward myself. Nothing was as gratifying as the feeling of the starch splashing against my face. I took the thick, heavy potato cutter that shaped them like waffle fries and slammed it down against the potatoes in all different directions, causing slices of potato to fly everywhere.

I'd walk over to the stove and watch the oil glistening in the pan. My dad would instruct me to put in one piece of potato, but it would just fall to the bottom and stick there. The oil was never ready yet. I'd wait a little longer, and then I'd drop another slice of potato in the oil and watch it sink to the bottom and then sizzle up to the top, feeling a surge of excitement as it fried.

I did the whole batch, adding one slice at a time. Then I laid paper towels on a plate and spooned the fries out. I could almost hear Nana Mae saying, "Kosher salt! Kosher salt!" as I quickly sprinkled them. And then we all enjoyed our delicious, salty, crunchy-on-the-outside and soft-on-the-inside French fries. I didn't think anything could be better than that.

I made a mess when I was cooking, not on purpose but just because I had so much extra energy that sometimes food spilled onto the countertops . . . and onto the floor . . . and even the walls. My mom would go ballistic when this happened. She took a lot of pride in our home and wanted the house to be perfectly polished and clean at all times. My mother wouldn't go to sleep if she knew there was a dish left in the sink. Sometimes I'd wake up in the middle of the night to hear the sound of a vacuum running or furniture being rearranged.

We weren't allowed to eat fish in the house because my mom didn't want the house to smell, but I was allowed to have tuna as long as I drained the can in the sink, cleaned out the can with soap and water, and then immediately took the trash out and cleaned the sink with bleach. We had one wooden bowl that was specifically designated for making tuna salad. My mom had strict rules about that kind of stuff, but my dad just did what he wanted.

One morning he grabbed the wooden bowl at random, put eggs, milk, and pancake mix in there, and handed it to me to start whisking. My mom came into the room and gasped in horror. "Jesse! What are you doing?" she cried. "Not that bowl!" My parents started bickering, which made me feel uneasy, but my dad just laughed it off. "Calm down, Randi," he said, which never succeeded in calming her down. He got out the big stovetop griddle and plugged it in. I turned it up to high and poured a capful of oil onto the surface, full of anticipation as I watched it sizzle. My dad poured some batter onto the griddle, and I was so excited that I flipped the first pancake too soon. Batter splattered everywhere. "Jesse!" My mother started yelling at me again, furious that I was making a mess.

But strangely, as angry as she got, she never made me clean up after myself. Sure, my mom asked me to do routine chores. I can still hear her voice saying, "Clean your room," or "Take out the garbage," but I learned from an early age how to get out of it. I became a master manipulator, at least when it came to my parents. Just when it was time to clear the dinner table, I'd disappear into the bathroom for an hour and leave my sister to deal with the mess. Or I'd come up with one excuse or another for why I couldn't do it.

At some point my parents must have just given up, because they simply stopped asking. My entire childhood passed without me ever having to set the dinner table, take out the trash, vacuum a carpet, or clean a bathroom, and I learned that it was possible to get away with just about anything. My parents never attached consequences to my behavior. They never set rules, and when they did they didn't enforce them. My parents loved Joee and me. They wanted us to be happy. So they smoothed everything over, doing everything they could to avoid conflict and constantly trying to placate us.

If my mother had had her way, we kids would have been disciplined more. My parents were never on the same page when it came to laying down the law. It was like a cat-and-mouse game between the two of them, and I quickly learned how to play this game to my full advantage. My mother would tell us to pick up our toys, do our homework, or call our grandparents, and behind her back my dad would tell me, "Don't worry about what she says. Just do what she wants and make her happy." So I forced out some crocodile tears or said "yes" to my mother if it would help me avoid confrontation or get me what I wanted. But I never adjusted my behavior because I knew at the end of the day there would be no repercussions.

Both of my parents cared a lot about image, especially my mom. She used to show up to my soccer games decked out in designer clothes and high heels, while all the other mothers would come in sweats and T-shirts. My mom stood out, and I already felt like an outsider. The other kids teased me. "Dude, your mom's hot," they would say. I hated hearing that. I just wished she'd put on some fucking mom jeans or something. But she always wanted to look her best. It wasn't just her looks that made my mom stand out. She was always the first to volunteer to be on the board of a charity or run a fund-raiser. Now I can appreciate how giving she is of her time, but as a kid who just wanted to fit in, my mom's conspicuousness bothered me.

Joee and I absorbed the message that looks were important, and over time we learned how to stuff everything down and act like we had no problems. For a kid as full of angst as me, this was a dangerous combination. I never learned how to deal with my feelings. For the time being, cooking was a productive outlet, but the restlessness simmered and would eventually find another way out.

As soon as I started school I was breaking the rules. I was the class clown for sure, bored, restless, and looking for a distraction to break the monotony. I whispered lewd jokes to my friends and ignored the teacher when she called my name just to see what she would do. I was only in the first grade when I was suspended for mooning the bus driver. But I was never punished at home. I apologized, pled my case, and managed to manipulate my way out of a punishment every time. And then I went ahead and did something equally disruptive again. I had zero fear of authority. If anything, I liked the attention that came with acting out.

Some of this behavior was intentional, but there were times when I couldn't control it. When I was still in the first grade, I went to get a haircut and was moving around in the seat so much that the hairdresser cut himself and had to get stitches. My mother was furious, but it wasn't like I did it on purpose. I just couldn't sit still.

Sometimes my dad's parents, Grandma Rosie and Grandpa Laz, picked up Joee and me from school and brought us back to their apartment. Then I could leave the class clown act behind at school and focus on having fun in the kitchen. Grandma Rosie picked up where Nana Mae had left off teaching me to cook. She was always making something interesting and was eager for me to hang out in the kitchen with her and help.

The day before Passover, Grandma Rosie made split pea soup with flanken bones, the Jewish version of short ribs. She had a little stool for me that she pulled up to her stove, which was an old electric coil one. Then, as she worked, I slid the stool across the tile floor to go fetch her ingredients. I climbed up and used all my might to pull open the freezer door and grab the frozen peas. But the best part was when I pushed the stool over to the stainless steel sink, rolled up my sleeves, and rinsed the peas, thawing them in the colander. I still remember the feeling of the peas between my fingers.

I sat down on my stool and cut the carrots, feeling the warmth at my back as Grandma Rosie stirred a large pot. She bent down to grab the vegetables from me, pausing to touch my face. "I love spending this time with you, Jesse," she said lovingly. These weren't words I heard often. Finally the moment came when I stood on my stool to dump the colander of peas into the pot. The steam hit my face as the peas joined the onions and carrots. I took the wooden spoon, and with Rosie's hand wrapped around mine, we stirred and stirred and stirred the soup, adding the flanken bones one by one.

Grandpa Laz had a La-Z-Boy that he sat in to watch the news with a newspaper in one hand and a Dewar's in the other, and while the peas cooked I'd climb up and sit on his lap. After hours of cooking, the peas stewed down with the flanken bones, transforming into a rich, delicious soup. But it was always better the next day, when we brought it to my parents' house. The whole extended family ate the soup, and when they said how much they loved it, I felt truly proud of myself for the first time.

My parents were always looking for opportunities for Joee and me to experience something new and broaden our horizons. When I was nine years old we went on a trip to Israel with our synagogue. It was amazing to see a place that was so completely different from where we lived. Joee was a cool preteen by then, and I looked up to her. When she went out with her friends in Tel Aviv I begged her to let me tag along, but I was the annoying little brother and she never wanted to hang out with me.

In addition to our regular family trips, for every summer for as long as I can remember, my parents sent Joee and me on a trip of our own. First we visited their friends Arthur and Joanie in Copake Lake in the Berkshires. We loved it there. Arthur and my dad grew up together in Brooklyn. He and Joanie were like my parents, but they weren't my parents. They were fun-loving and open.

From Copake Lake, Joee and I made our way down to New Paltz, a small town in the Hudson Valley, to stay with my uncle Bruce and aunt Stacey and my cousins Bonnie, Jonah, Sean, and Keith. Their house at 35 Gatehouse Road was our home for the month of June. For Joee and me, it wasn't just a house but a magic fucking castle. The house had an amazing wraparound deck, and out back were massive, fingerprint-stained double-glass doors that led into a playroom filled with every conceivable piece of shit kids love: miniature pianos, tennis rackets, baseball gloves, hockey sticks, action figures, board games, and an eight-track player. On a far brick wall, collecting dust, was an unused woodstove. The floor was covered with a furry gray carpet that had cushioned countless amateur wrestling matches and impromptu martial arts exhibitions.

The backyard was a wild, unkempt country wonderland with a pond, a big white rock, a sprawling rosebush, and a gnarled old birch tree that presided like a standing sentry. We spent a lot of time in that wild backyard hunting frogs, catching crayfish, getting dirty, skipping stones, and wreaking havoc.

My oldest cousin, Bonnie, had already moved out, so every June there were five kids living at 35 Gatehouse Road, all of us boys except for Joee. I was the youngest, and I loved being around my cousins, who were all kick-ass high school wrestlers. They were like the older brothers I never had.

Sean, the oldest, was a musician; he sent me my first mix tape and heavily influenced my taste in music as I was growing up. Jonah, the middle child, was the family survivalist. You could drop him in the middle of a zombie apocalypse with just a Bowie knife and he'd pull through, no problem. His specialty was climbing the Gunks, a twelve-mile-long, 300-foot-high escarpment that towered over open fields and farmlands. He was like a billy goat, and I marveled at his effortless movement over the steep rocks. Camped out a couple of hundred feet high on a ledge overlooking a vast expanse of the Hudson Valley, we spent hours just staring up at the sky. Like me, Jonah had boundless energy, which he was able to channel into creative projects. And he was funny. He knew intuitively how to snap me out of a bad mood with a joke, and he still does. It didn't hurt that he had a hot girlfriend who followed him everywhere like a lost puppy.

But I was closest to Keith, the youngest, who is four years older than me. Like his brothers, Keith was a badass, three-time New York State high school wrestling champ. His room was covered in overlapping posters of '90s grunge rock gods like Layne Staley, Eddie Vedder, and Chris Cornell. I remember falling asleep on his floor listening to Alice in Chains' iconic album *Jar of Flies* and Faith No More's classic song "Epic."

"We're going to be in a band. You play the drums, I'll

play guitar," Keith told me again and again. Keith and I were close, more like brothers than cousins. We were always together. He brought me along to hang out with his friends, and before long his group became my group. Keith changed my life.

I idolized my aunt and uncle. Uncle Bruce could do anything with a card deck—deal from the bottom of the pack or cut the deck with a fake thumb. He was magical and embodied all of the qualities I admired. I went fishing with him in the Wallkill River because I wanted to, not because he pushed me to. I remember watching him, hunched over a table as he put the finishing touches on his handmade lures. On a good day we could reel in fifteen to twenty fish. He nurtured through exposure. Uncle Bruce was my dad without the baggage of actually being my dad. I guess that's exactly what uncles are supposed to be.

Aunt Stacey was hip. She was tall with flowing red hair and a hint of freckles on her skin. She always wore cool beaded jewelry and dressed in flowery skirts. And she loved to garden. There were rock piles in front of the house that she turned into beautiful flowerbeds. Aunt Stacey cultivated the earth, intuitively understood its potential, and worked in harmony with it. I understood this. I felt the same way anytime I stepped into a kitchen. Gardening and cooking were our spiritual activities. Aunt Stacey reminded me of the Oracle in the *Matrix* movies—a calm, sort of mysterious woman, but also a powerful figure who seemed perfectly content raising a family. I was able to really open up to Aunt Stacey, who was engaged, present, patient, and emotionally available. In New Paltz we also loved spending time with my uncle Sam, my dad's younger brother, and my aunt Janet. They were more like friends than parental figures and were always cool to hang out with.

Despite how laid-back my aunt and uncle were (or maybe because of it), 35 Gatehouse Road was a circus. It was messy and disorganized—a 180-degree shift from our house in Parkland. Keith described it as "organized chaos," which was spot-on. But somehow it all worked. My aunt Stacey cooked more than my mother, making simple, hearty dishes like a giant pot of chicken soup or a meatloaf that we kids could feel free to attack whenever we felt like it.

In contrast to the organized chaos of the house was the quiet outside. New Paltz is really fucking quiet. Sometimes at night I just paused and listened to the wind rustling the leaves of some old, wobbly-looking trees, crickets chirping— the typical sounds of country living. On warm summer evenings local residents were out and about, walking along the town's cobblestone sidewalks or navigating the maze of Revolutionary-era carriage roads. But mostly I remember New Paltz for its pristine forests, rolling fields, rushing creeks, nature trails thick with stinging insects, and the loss of innocence.

CHAPTER TWO

Coddle

Coddle: A method of cooking eggs by cracking them into a small buttered dish or ramekin with a lid, adding seasonings, and then partially immersing the dish in near-boiling water for several minutes.

I was twelve years old in 1994. On a Friday night in late June a summer moon peeked through the light silvery clouds as my cousin Keith and I made the rounds through New Paltz. He had turned sixteen that year, so this was the first summer he could drive, and we navigated our way down a dark, leaf- and branch-strewn road in his red Toyota Tercel, which had been handed down through his family. In the distance, a faint sound beckoned, a low, synthesized bass that beat like an anxious heart. I knew that rhythm all too well.

I had always thought that rave music was kind of meaningless and repetitive. I am, and always have been, an alternative rock guy all the way. But that night the relentless beat called to me. The freedom it represented was intoxicating. Ten minutes later Keith and I were surrounded by dizzying lights, deafening music, and a bunch of kids like us who were also looking for a break from reality.

At that point drugs weren't on my radar, but when the

group of guys Keith and I were talking to started passing around a joint, I didn't hesitate. I took my cues from Keith and watched how it was done as he grabbed the joint and took a hit. I felt giddy, full of excitement and nervous energy, like the first time I kissed a girl. When my turn came and I took a drag, my lips were so dry they stuck to the joint. Then I immediately started coughing. My chest hurt. It wasn't what I had expected. But then, as soon as I stopped coughing, it felt as though a part of myself had suddenly been lifted away. Ever since I was a baby peeling wallpaper from the walls of my room, I had never been able to get rid of that twitchy, anxious part of me. The big wool blanket that I'd been carrying around my whole life like a fucking disease suddenly lifted, and that feeling trumped any escape I'd previously found through acting out, clowning around, or even cooking.

I went into that rave as one person and came out another. Deep down I knew that a metamorphosis had taken place. I had turned into a pickle and would never be a cucumber again. The innocence was gone. I was changed forever. And there was no turning back.

For the next year my life completely revolved around cooking and getting stoned, often at the same time. Back in Parkland, I started acting funny. I was always on the lookout for pot, desperate to re-create that feeling of ease I'd experienced at the rave. It didn't take long for me to figure out that alcohol helped. I started stealing my parents' booze and hanging out with older kids who had access, hiding out in the woods and smoking joints we rolled using dollar bills. One of the older kids I hung out with was Sam, who was always getting in trouble for one thing or another. I looked up to Sam in a weird way. He was tough and intimidating and taught me by example how to hold my own in any situation.

If my parents noticed the change in me, they never said anything. But it wasn't long before I was hanging out with an entirely new crowd. One of those new friends was Mike Charnam, a formerly pudgy kid I had known since Little League who was now a cocky, confident teenager who wore Slayer and Metallica T-shirts and torn jeans and rode around on a blue dirt bike loaded with decals. Girls were always hanging around Charnam, and he knew all the cool kids. A group of us started sitting in the back of the school bus together, always causing some sort of trouble: Andre, Charnam, and me.

After school we often retreated to my backyard or sat by the Cypress Head lake smoking cigarettes and listening to music. Though I was heavily into pot, I still held on to my interest in food. My dresser drawers were stuffed with menus alongside rolling papers, pipes, and matches. I raced home after school, arriving just in time to watch *Great Chefs, Great Cities*. Other times, Charnam and I ditched school just to watch *Iron Chef America*. Food and pot became part of our shared experience. We pitch a couple of tents by the lake, have a barbecue, and get loaded.

Other times we invaded my kitchen. One day all of us, maybe five or six guys, were smoking pot at my house when I decided to make a feast for everybody of grilled cheeses and cream soda floats. I got the cream sodas out of the fridge and put them in the blender with some ice cream. While they were still going, I started fucking around and released my hold on the top of the blender. Cream soda went everywhere, especially all over my friend Mike's face. He picked up another can of soda from the counter, shook it up, and then sprayed it all over me. The next thing I knew we were embroiled in a huge cream soda fight, and the sticky substance was bubbling from the ceiling, the floor, the cabinets, and was all over us. The mess didn't bother me. I just continued cooking the grilled cheeses with bacon and mixing together barbecue sauce and ketchup to go on top.

Of course my mom went nuts when she saw the kitchen, but I pleaded and cajoled my way out of a punishment and didn't even have to clean up the mess. I never felt guilty for making her clean up after me. Maybe deep down I was trying to get back at her for the way her obsession with looks made me feel. It was around that hormone-fueled age when her appearance really started to bother me. I was messing around in the kitchen with some friends another time when my mom came downstairs all dressed up to go out. She had on these skintight pants and high-heeled stiletto boots, with bright lipstick and her hair all done up. My friends were staring at her and giving me shit, talking about her body. My mom was beautiful, but who wants their friends to look at their mother that way?

My parents tried their best to control me the only way they knew how—by managing my appearance. As if scratching the surface would have made a difference. I became friends with some skateboard kids who wore jeans with holes and shirts embroidered with band logos. I wanted to get piercings, but my dad hated all of that. "Those are bad kids," he told me. "You're just asking for trouble if you walk around looking like that."

But the truth is, I *was* looking for trouble. I kept pushing the boundaries and never bumped up against any consequences, so I just kept pushing harder. By the end of seventh grade I was smoking pot every day. There was a silent, malevolent force driving my behavior that compelled me to keep pushing the envelope. In a way, Charnam was my safeguard because he never went further than pot or booze, but nothing was off-limits for me.

I celebrated my bar mitzvah that year. The religious aspects of Judaism never clicked with me, but I loved the traditions and the feeling of camaraderie that came with sitting around the table with my family at Passover and other holidays. I loved being a part of that fun-loving, close-knit Schenker clan. My mom's younger sister, my aunt Stacey, and my uncle Mark were always at the house hanging out with us, and I looked forward to family gatherings. It's customary at a bar mitzvah reception to have your loved ones come up to the podium and each light a special candle, and I called my dad up to light what I called a "best friend" candle. But I didn't need a best friend. I needed a parent.

With my inhibitions down and hormones raging, my interest in girls suddenly picked up. It was Charnam, in fact, who introduced me to my first girlfriend. Jen was a year younger than me, with wavy brown hair, dark eyes, and an infectious giggle. I was smitten.

At first Jen and I just made small talk. I was only twelve and didn't have the nerve to do much else. Charnam broke the ice by hanging out with Jen, her friend Katy, and me after school. He attached a cart to his dirt bike and pulled Katy and Jen around Cypress Head. At that point the only two things I was interested in were pot and cooking. But I couldn't smoke (or cook, really) all day long. Jen filled the void. She also probably slowed down the snowball, as even my interest in pot waned a bit when I was around her. Somehow Jen was able to fill the hole—that relentless, empty feeling that followed me everywhere. I felt good around her. I liked myself in the relationship because I had integrity. There was no plotting or scheming. I never tried to manipulate her the way I did my parents and teachers.

Before long Jen and I were going home together, usually to her house since both of her parents worked and were rarely home. At night I'd cut through the bushes to get to her street, which was just a few blocks away, and sneak in her window. Jen positioned her mattress close to the wall so I could hide in the space between the wall and the mattress if her parents ever walked in.

For the next year and a half, Jen and I were inseparable. We spent hours making out and exploring each other's bodies. We never spoke about it, but the next step was becoming abundantly clear.

One Friday afternoon I walked into a drugstore and stole a box of condoms. My parents had split for the weekend, and Joee was gone. Jen and I started out in my bedroom, rolling around on my bed with our legs intertwined. Slowly, I moved my hand up her shirt, unbuttoned her bra, and started squeezing her breasts. We were both shaking with excitement. Somehow we ended up in the guest room, where I laid her down on the bed and slowly started to undress her. We had gone this far before, but this time it was different. With Pearl Jam's "Indifference" blaring in the background, I lost my virginity.

Just when my relationship with Jen was picking up, I had to contend with an entirely new experience—loss—when my Grandma Rosie lost a long battle with brain cancer. Of course my Nana Mae had already died, but I was so young when she passed away, and she was quite old. With Rosie, it was different. A wave of sadness like I'd never experienced before ran through our house. I can still remember the look of pure despair on my Grandpa Laz's face. I'd loved Rosie too. I didn't know how to process my emotions, so I found another place to stuff my grief.

I poured myself into cooking even more, no longer just experimenting but actually creating. Some of these creations were spectacular failures, like the chicken I marinated in blackberries with Coca-Cola and garlic that was totally inedible. But the more I practiced the more I finally started to make things that tasted good. One weekend my buddy Fred and I took some soft challah bread my mom had sitting around and stuffed it with creamy peanut butter and jelly. Then we soaked the whole thing in eggs, cream, sugar, and the slightest hint of vanilla. We pan-fried it until the edges turned crispy but the inside stayed gooey and creamy. Picture a grilled cheese sandwich, but with warm peanut butter and jelly inside instead of cheese. It took a few attempts to get it exactly right, but when we did we had created the perfect stoner sandwich. Of course, this creation later became one of Recette's signature brunch dishes, PB&J Pain Perdu.

Before long it seemed like everyone in Parkland knew

about the PB&J. My parents often went out for dinner with their friends and then came home and asked me to make it for them for dessert. But that wasn't enough for me. I wanted to learn everything I could about food—what dishes they served in restaurants and how the chefs made them work. I started reading restaurant reviews in the *Sun Sentinel* each week, selecting a restaurant for my parents to go to. Then I'd ask them to bring me back a menu. At home I studied those menus with a focus I never had for schoolwork. I was eager to learn every detail of those recipes so I could take them to the next level by creating something of my own.

After we'd been together for a year and a half, Jen left me for a high school senior. We had been hanging out less and less for a while, so I sensed it coming, but nothing could have prepared me for the loss of my first love. She called it off over the phone. "I don't know about this anymore, Jess," she told me. "I think I need some time." And that was it. She hung up, and it felt like a punch to the gut. I sat on the edge of my bed for the next few hours crying like an infant. Jen had been the perfect distraction from my anxiety, and once she was gone it came rushing back, only now with a vengeance.

That's when things changed for me. When I was fourteen, I started hanging out with two guys named Chris and Riley. Chris lived in a nearby town, Coral Springs. Chris was privileged. We all were. Parkland and parts of Coral Springs were crammed with oversize McMansions that were designed to look like fancy chateaus, farmhouses, and Renaissance palazzos. I was lucky to grow up in such a close and loving family, but with my new friends I formed my own identity by rebelling against the privilege I'd been raised with. Riding skateboards, vandalizing property, smoking cigarettes, getting high, causing mayhem—we'd do anything we thought would piss off our parents.

Riley was a couple of years older than me and Chris, and he had a car. In our minds this represented freedom. Chris and I snuck out at night, and then Riley and one of his friends would pick us up down the road, out of view of our parents. Then we'd drive around for hours, smoking weed and causing trouble.

Fourteen years old and hooked on pot—at a certain point money became a problem for me. I got a job at McDonald's, but seven bucks an hour wasn't enough to support my burgeoning drug habit. Chris solved the problem by filching a couple hundred bucks from his parents. That night Riley and his friend took us to meet a dealer. We parlayed Chris's windfall into four ounces of weed, which was a shitload for two reckless fourteen-year-olds who already thought they owned the fucking world. I kept the stash in my backpack. We smoked most of it ourselves and sold some to the other kids at school. There we were: two baby-faced pot dealers. As kids clamored around us in the hallways, looking to score, I had never felt so popular or important. In my own way, I finally fit in.

With tennis courts, a volleyball net, a pool, and a basketball court, the Cypress Head clubhouse was a gathering place for residents on the lake. In back of the clubhouse was a massive deck that was used for parties. The lake was stocked with bass, and you could fish off the deck. A massive overhang covered the deck, so no one could see what you were doing, especially after dark. It was the perfect place to finger some chick, vandalize property, or get stoned.

Pot goes quickly when you use every day. After a week, Chris and I had nearly reached the end of our four ounces, and we agreed to meet up on the clubhouse deck to smoke the rest. We loaded our Pyrex pipe with some of the remaining weed and sat on the deck with our backs to its two entrances, puffing away. Suddenly, in a blur, cops swarmed in from both sides. "Stop what you're doing now!" a gruff, faceless voice called out from the darkness.

I quickly grabbed the bag with the remaining weed and threw it in a patch of lakeside weeds. But the cops were faster than me. They grabbed Chris and me, slapped cuffs on our wrists, and sat us in the back of a squad car. Strangely enough, I wasn't worried about getting busted by the cops as I sat there. Instead, I felt a sort of perverse excitement about being arrested. The feeling of those cuffs on my wrists and the cheap leather of the squad car seat against the backs of my legs was oddly empowering. All I could think was, *Wow. This is fucking cool.*

Being arrested made me feel special, fueling my overblown fourteen-year-old ego and adding another layer to my already thick sense of entitlement. I knew I could manipulate my parents and that nothing would come of this incident. As usual, there would be no consequences. They loved me too much to watch me suffer. No one was shipping me off to military school or abandoning me, and I knew there was a safety net in place, no matter what, to catch my fall. At the Parkland Police Department headquarters, my hands were cuffed to the back of a cold gray office chair. It was my first arrest: possession of a controlled substance.

My dad didn't impose any limits on me, but he was still a powerful force in my life. I admired my dad and looked up to him. He got angry whenever I fell short of his high expectations of me, which happened all the time. Deep down I didn't think I would ever live up to his standards, so I didn't even try. The look of disgust and anger on his face when he came into the station that night was far more difficult for me to deal with than any arrest. The drive from the Parkland police station to our house took only a few minutes, but on that night it seemed like an eternity. It was eerily silent, with none of the usual banter about music or sports. I don't think my dad knew what to say or what to do with me. Parkland is a small town, and my dad was active in the community. My behavior made him look like a failure, and he must've felt ashamed, vulnerable, and defenseless.

As soon as we got home I launched into all of my usual bullshit. I played the victim, cried some well-timed tears, and threw in a touch of remorse to top it off. This was the best, most fail-safe recipe I had created to date, and it worked like a charm. "It's just a phase," I heard my dad say to my mother later that night. As soon as I heard that I knew for sure that there would be no consequences. I lay in bed that night with a single thought dominating my consciousness. I didn't think about getting arrested. I didn't worry about parental repercussions, public scorn, or even what anyone thought about my behavior. All I could think about was getting high again.

My parents sent me to a psychologist for an evaluation after that first arrest. To me, this was a small price to pay. The therapist's name was Alan Braunstein, and his office smelled like patchouli oil and eucalyptus. Pictures of Bob Dylan and Jerry Garcia lined the walls. I grew up listening to that music and felt right at home. At my first appointment Alan gave me all these tests to take, the kind where I had to tell him what I saw in a picture. He liked me, I could tell, and I was honest with Alan. I didn't feel the need to lie to him or manipulate him, at least not yet. I vividly described the way pot made me feel and what it did for me. He didn't judge; he just listened. Afterward he told my parents that I was intelligent and had real talent, but that I needed long-term rehab. He believed that the way I responded to the drug was a warning sign and a harbinger of bad things to come but my parents brushed it off. They didn't want to believe that I had a real problem, so they told themselves, "He's just experimenting. It's normal."

Just a few months later I boarded the school bus feeling giddy. I had about half an ounce of some really good shit in my pocket and plans to meet up with some kids after school to get wasted. But suddenly I realized that walking into school with a wad of pot in my pocket wasn't such a great idea. Weed fucking reeks, especially the good stuff, and the teachers would be able to smell me coming from down the hallway. I reached into my backpack and pulled out a cassette tape of Alice in Chains' *Jar of Flies*—the perfect place to store weed. I quickly scanned the busybodies in the hallway and then carefully pulled a sandwich-sized bag out of my right front pocket, took out the cassette, and meticulously placed the pot inside the cassette tape case. Just as I was about to return the case to my backpack I noticed a raggedy-looking kid with a mop of curly brown hair wearing glasses.

He was staring right at me for God only knows how long. I was so fixated on hiding the weed that I didn't even notice him, but he must've seen the whole thing go down. Still, I shrugged it off, figuring there was no way he was going to rat me out.

The morning rolled by. A couple of hours had passed since the incident in the hallway, and it already seemed like a distant memory. By third period I was sitting in the back of English class, flirting with a cute girl. I was hardly paying attention to whatever the teacher was talking about when one of the school administrators materialized at the classroom door. After whispering in the teacher's ear, she made her way to the back of the classroom and stopped right in front of my desk. "Jesse Schenker," she said in a detached drawl, "take your things and come with me."

I immediately knew what had happened. That kid had ratted me out. But rather than feeling scared, I actually felt special in a strange way. I had no idea what was going to happen to me, but things were definitely about to get interesting. We arrived at the principal's office, and the administrator slowly opened the door. Standing next to the principal was a cop. "Jesse, hand over your backpack," the principal demanded.

The cop started rummaging through my backpack. All I could do was sit there and watch. Moments later he pulled out the tape. He knew exactly what he was looking for. "Jesse, take a seat," the principal said and then proceeded to call my parents. As always, I was concerned about my dad's reaction, but I knew that nothing was really going to happen to me. My dad knew how to work the system even better than I did. No matter where we went, we never waited on line. My dad would tip the maître d' at a hot restaurant or the security guard at a concert and we'd walk right in. He knew how the world worked, and greasing the wheels had a lot to do with it. I don't know what he said to that cop, but the charges against me were dropped. All I had to do was write a letter of apology. My parents were more concerned about the fact that the principal wanted to expel me, but after several hours of begging I ended up with only a week's suspension.

My parents were both visibly upset when we got home. I wondered if they regretted ignoring Alan Braunstein's advice after our first appointment and would now take it more seriously. The three of us sat down, and right on cue I cried a few tears and told my parents how sorry I was and all the usual bullshit. No one was better at faking remorse than me, and they bought it hook, line, and sinker. I ended up serving my week of suspension on a family vacation in Aspen.

Years later a therapist asked me what I learned from that experience. I never answered his question, but to me it was obvious. I learned that I could get away with anything. My grandfather used to say that my sister and I were the only kids he knew who got rewarded for what they didn't do.

CHAPTER THREE

Roulade

Roulade: Originating from the French *rouler*, meaning "to roll," a roulade is a dish consisting of a slice of meat or other protein rolled around a filling, such as cheese, vegetables, or other meats.

Cate was tall and slim, and she had mesmerizing big blue eyes. She was quirky and kind of offbeat, but damn if she couldn't make me laugh. By freshman year of high school we were inseparable. By then I'd also been smoking pot nonstop for two years, and the need for a constant supply consumed me. All day, every day, I searched for weed. Luckily, Cate had a neighbor named Simon with a steady supply. Most days after school I went straight from the school bus to Simon's and then to Cate's house, where we spent the afternoon smoking, getting high, playing golf, and listening to music. At night Cate and I retreated out to her porch and spent hours just gazing at the sky and following the stars.

The best source for pot in Parkland was Simon's brother Josh. He was a couple of years older than me and as big as a small elephant. And he had a car. In October, Josh, Cate, and I were driving down Lyon's Road in Coconut Creek when Josh ran a stop sign and a cop pulled up behind us. On cue, Josh grabbed his stash and stuffed it under his gut. He was so big that he could hide his weed under the thick roll of fat around his middle. I was in the backseat with a pipe and a little bit of pot, which I immediately crammed into my right sock.

"Get out of the car," the cop ordered. As we got out he asked Josh, "You got any drugs?" He began to search Josh, but even Sherlock Holmes wouldn't have been able to find anything under all that blubber. The cop and his partner let Josh go. Then the police started searching me. I considered confessing, but was too scared. These were county officers, not the rinky-dink cops who'd busted me in the past. The cop found the stash in my sock within two minutes and immediately slapped some plastic cuffs on my wrists.

"Sit on the curb and wait there," he ordered. A couple of minutes later Josh and Cate left. She offered to stay with me, but there was no need for her to make the trip. This was my fucking deal.

They took me down to the precinct, put me in a cell, and handcuffed me to a pipe. I was freaking out, thinking for sure there'd be serious consequences this time. It was my third arrest in three years, and even my dad couldn't bail me out of trouble this time because I had a prior record. As it turned out, we had to get a lawyer, and I went before a judge, who handed me a sentence of fifty hours of community service like she was giving out candy. I'd also have to check in with a probation officer once a month.

Through some friend of a friend, my father found a shelter for battered women that needed help from volunteers. We drove over to the secluded place and met with the woman in charge. At one point my dad asked me to leave the room, and he closed the door behind me; then he emerged a few minutes later, without saying a word. Within a week I received a letter in the mail with all of my community service paperwork already filled out. To this day I have no idea what went on behind that door, but I know I never had to do a day of community service.

Every time I got arrested my parents took me straight to Alan's office. It was always the same drill. They had me sit in the therapist's seat and sat with Alan on the couch; then the three of them grilled me for an hour. It was always intense and emotional as we cried together and came up with a game plan and consequences. But as soon as we got home everything would go back to the status quo.

Alan was a good therapist. He saw right through my act and knew I needed serious treatment, but my parents didn't want to hear it.

At that point the status quo consisted of smoking pot every day, cooking every chance I got, and studying food through cooking shows, restaurant menus, and eventually cookbooks. One day I saw a chef on TV slicing artichokes paper-thin, and I became obsessed with learning how to do that. I convinced my parents to buy me some artichokes, but when they brought the mysterious, thorny vegetables home, I had no idea where to start. Finally, I decided to put the artichokes in the freezer, figuring it would be easier to slice them frozen. It was a spectacular failure, with artichoke pieces flying everywhere, but it was the start of my learning how to manipulate ingredients.

When I was a young kid, my dad pushed me to try just

about every sport imaginable—baseball, flag football, soccer, and one year I even tried basketball. Despite his busy work schedule he found the time to coach every single one of my teams. Baseball was the only one I really enjoyed or was any good at. I did have a live arm, and maybe if I'd had the motivation I'd have been pretty good. But my growing commitment to marijuana ensured that I didn't make the high school team when I tried out that year. That was fine with me. When I was younger I loved playing sports with my dad, but as a rebellious teen I wanted to get out from under his thumb. Not making the team was the perfect excuse to stop playing. There I was— young, full of nervous energy, with no respect for boundaries and a lot of extra time on my hands. I filled the void with pot, cooking, music, and sex.

When Cate's parents went out and she was stuck babysitting her little brother, I would go over to her house, and after he was asleep I'd raid the fridge, excited to find new ingredients to experiment with. One night I used squash and corn to make a crazy version of shepherd's pie that I covered with cheese and breadcrumbs and baked until it was golden brown and the cheese was bubbling up like lava. The excitement of creating something that delicious was better than any high I'd experienced so far.

Cate and I also found ourselves alone in my house a lot. My parents would go out of town and leave Joee in charge, but she was no angel either and threw parties for her friends. I'd invite my own crew over, and we'd drink beer and smoke weed until 2:00 or 3:00 A.M., when one of our neighbors would inevitably call the police. Over time those Schenker house parties became the stuff of legend.

One night Cate and I moved into my parents' bathroom, a quiet place for us to chill. There was a deep pink tub surrounded by gleaming black tiles and adorned with little soap dishes and bottles filled with sweet-smelling oils and beads. Cate sat in the empty tub while I took up residence on the edge. We silently passed a bong back and forth, something we'd done dozens of other times. But this time something wasn't right. Finally it hit me. I was high, but I still felt the anxiety. The emptiness and anxiety were back; they were there even while I was smoking. This had never happened before. It struck me that pot was no longer enough to fill the gaping hole inside me.

It was 1:00 or 2:00 in the morning by the time Cate finally fell asleep. After I knew she was out, I went into my parents' medicine cabinet and swallowed six Benadryl. I didn't know what I was doing. But I had to do something to change the way I was feeling. The Benadryl didn't get me high. There was no euphoria, no pink cloud or white fucking elephant. I just passed out. But within a week over-the-counter meds were part of my new routine. Nyquil, Benadryl, Tylenol PM, Robitussin—nothing was off-limits.

One day I came home and found Joee sprawled on the floor of our parents' bedroom. "Jesse, I feel like shit. I think I'm going to puke," she mumbled. That afternoon Joee had had her wisdom teeth removed, and she was in a lot of pain. I lifted her up and moved her onto the bed. Her face was red and swollen. She felt warm to the touch and was probably running a fever. She could barely speak. I tried to make her laugh by making fun of our parents—this was how we always bonded. As we were talking I noticed an orange plastic bottle with a gleaming white cap sitting on my mother's nightstand.

My search was over, at least for the moment. As soon as Joee fell asleep I snagged one of her five-milligram doses of oxycodone. Ten minutes later I was superman. The feeling of warmth started in the pit of my stomach and spread quickly throughout my entire body. As it spread all of my discomfort, anxiety, and ambivalence slowly washed away.

Before long the first thing I asked whenever entering someone's home was, "May I use your bathroom?" No, I didn't want to take a leak. I didn't want to wash my hands or blow my fucking nose. I was only interested in separating people from the contents of their medicine cabinets. I quickly found that neurotic Jewish mothers had the best stuff. I often found little cases filled with an assortment of unmarked pills. Sometimes I had no idea what I was taking, but that little fact didn't stop me. If I got worried, I called the Poison Control Center and pretended to be a parent whose kid had accidentally swallowed a pill.

"Can you help me? My son just swallowed a blue, oval-shaped pill with a line through the middle."

"Sir, that's an anti-inflammatory. You can relax."

Once I saw what that single oxycodone could do, it became my singular mission to find opiates—Percocet, Darvocet, hydrocodone, hydromorphone, or morphine. I wasn't picky. These were my new drug of choice, my go-to way of filling the void and finding peace. Nothing relieves emptiness like opiates.

In eleventh grade I started attending Atlantic Technical Center and Technical High School, a massive place just ten minutes from my parents' house with thousands of students spread out over twenty different buildings. Housed in one of those ugly pink buildings was the Culinary Arts Program. Five mornings a week I attended classes there from 7:15 to 10:45. Then I'd drive over to Marjory Stoneman Douglas High School for academic classes from 12:00 to 2:40.

Most people think of Atlantic Tech as a place for students who have zero interest in college or academics and just want to enter the workforce, but the culinary program was a little different. My classmates there ran the gamut from house-wives looking to pick up a new skill to older men who were on their third career. There were also plenty of kids like me, outcasts and misfits who naturally gravitated toward food. I connected with those kids in a way I never could have with the kids at my regular high school.

Jim Large was one of those kids who I clicked with right away. We met in my first course, "Sanitation and Safety." The nutritionist who taught the class was young, probably in her mid-twenties. She taught us things like the difference between simple and complex carbohydrates and safe food-handling procedures. I'd already learned a lot of this material from my McDonald's training, and Jim already had a gig cooking at one of the better restaurants in Coral Springs that I'll call Savannah. Despite the fact that he was short and chubby with stringy blond hair and glasses, his job and the fact that he had a car—a brand-new, bright yellow Jeep —made him a big deal around campus.

One day when I finished my shift at McDonald's and was walking out back, Jim pulled up in his Jeep. "Jump in," he called to me. "There's someone I want you to meet."

Jim took me straight to his boss at Savannah. "I got an

opening for a dishwasher," he said. I accepted the job right away. It was the perfect opportunity to watch, learn the line, and study the cooks. And it paid $7 an hour, 50 cents more than I was making at McDonald's.

My time at Savannah was baptism by fire. On my first night they were already short a cook. Jim approached me, looking a little nervous. "Can you help fry the calamari?" I was barely sixteen and I was manning the fry station at one of Broward County's hottest restaurants. Keeping up wasn't a problem. As I stood over the fryer that night with flour caked to my fingers and sweat pouring off my brow I learned something about myself: I wasn't just passionate about food—I was *good* at this.

But I was hired as a dishwasher, so after I fried my last calamari at midnight I made my way over to the dish pit, which was piled three feet high with dirty plates, pots, and pans. The garbage was overflowing, and huge globs of un-eaten food littered the floor. It was disgusting, and I had to clean it all up. It was my responsibility. But for some strange reason I loved it. It was a simple task to conquer, and a di-rect use of all my excess energy. It helped that I saw it as a sort of competition with Jim, who'd had the job before me. I wanted to do it faster and better than Jim ever did. It was only after I'd dragged all the dirty mats out to the back al-ley, cleaned each dish, mopped every inch of the floor, and thrown out every bit of trash that I finally allowed myself to breathe. My fingers were stained black, my apron was filthy, and my pants were caked thick with grease. My clothes, hair, and even skin reeked of fryer oil and the dirty grill. But I fucking loved it.

In a short time I became the best dishwasher and calamari fryer that Savannah had ever seen. But all along my addiction to marijuana and prescription pain pills was growing. I could feel the pull in two directions, between the serenity of the kitchen and the euphoria of the drugs. I was headed for the inevitable clash between them.

After "Safety and Sanitation" we moved on to the "Hot Foods" course taught by Chef Ball, a tall black guy in his fifties who Jim and I loved. When we were learning to flambé with brandy, he kept telling us to add more. We thought this was hilarious. Later that day Jim and I were in the back with some other guys, doing shots of brandy behind the #10 cans, when Chef Ball walked in and caught us. "Come here, guys," he said, bringing us into the kitchen. We thought we were in trouble, but then he said, "Let me teach you a trick." He pulled out some parsley and handed us each a sprig. "If you're ever out drinking and get pulled over driving home, chew on some of this. It gets rid of the smell." From that day on, Jim and I always had a sprig of parsley sticking out of our mouths. It was our way of tipping our hats to Chef Ball.

"Hot Foods" was where I learned the skills that took my creativity in the kitchen to a whole new level. I found learning about the five mother sauces—béchamel, velouté, espagnole or brown sauce, hollandaise, and tomato sauce—fascinating, but the velouté we learned to make, with its traditional roux, felt so old-fashioned to me. I started to play around with it, substituting oil and later chicken fat for the butter. It was around this time that I started obsessively collecting cookbooks. When I read about modern-day veloutés that were basically reductions without any flour, I realized that chefs really do have the license to take things in any direction they want. This was a lightbulb moment for me.

Now my creations at home were becoming more mature. I made pistachio nut–crusted salmon by grinding up pistachios, adding a bunch of butter, thyme, and garlic, and spreading this paste all over a cutting board. Then I put the salmon facedown in the paste, picked the whole thing up, and baked it in the oven. This might not have been groundbreaking in the culinary world, but it rocked my sixteen-year-old world. Despite my heavy level of partying, I never lost interest in experimenting in the kitchen. After parties, I always cooked gourmet meals for my friends and their families. Wherever I was when the keg was tapped, I went into the kitchen and made something with whatever ingredients I could find. One time the kitchen was bare except for a few basics, so I rolled out slices of Wonder Bread with a rolling pin, fried them in butter, and then made the ultimate tuna melt with tuna and cheddar cheese.

Jim eventually left Savannah to work at another hot local restaurant I'll call Graffiti, and I could feel my own time at Savannah coming to an end. I needed more. Before long I met Pete Etter, the executive chef at a happening restaurant in Boca that I'll call The Seawater Grill. Pete was an imposing guy, six-three or six-four and cue-ball bald except for two awkward patches of hair on each side of his head. He walked with a limp, always reeked of cigarettes, and wore nautical-themed shirts over his chef whites. Right away, he offered me a job making salads for $9 an hour.

After only one week at The Seawater Grill, Pete called me into a meeting in the restaurant's massive walk-in refrigerator. *Funny place for a meeting,* I thought to myself. I felt like I was about to relive some scene from a Mafia movie where I get whacked and the cops find my frozen body hanging by a hook a week later. "Jesse," Pete said to me, "I've never met anyone with more innate cooking talent than you. I picture you running your own kitchen someday. Just put your head down and keep your nose to the grindstone and you'll get there."

I don't know what motivated Pete to say that to me, but his words inspired me. Unknowingly, he'd thrown down a challenge. Now I had to be better than every other chef at Seawater. I came in earlier and stayed later than all the other employees. I tidied up the other chefs' stations when they were finished working, organized the walk-ins, and even helped the dishwashers clean the mats and mop the bathrooms at the end of the night.

By then we were in the "Cold Foods" section at school, learning our knife skills by chopping vegetables in an area of the kitchen that was kept so cold we had to wear two chef's coats. Chef Wilcock and I never got along, but in his class I really got into knife work. I loved using the melon baller to cut vegetables, and at home I started making perfectly circular carrots, wrapping them in blanched leeks, and tying them up with blanched pieces of chives. It was also in this class that I learned the terminology I needed to become a chef. I already knew what I was doing, but now I knew how to speak the language.

Before long a new food runner started work at Seawater. Dan was a few years older than me, probably twenty or twenty-one. He was movie-star handsome and muscular with a great sense of humor. Like Jim, he was someone

I hit if off with immediately. After work, Dan and I would sit on the hood of his car smoking joints and staring at the stars. "God, I'd love a Percocet right now," I said one night. Dan gave me a funny look. Then he started laughing, but didn't say a word. He went inside, and a few minutes later he walked out with David, the restaurant's main grill guy and a totally badass cook. David looked tough, with a tattoo of a half-naked chick on his left bicep and the rest of his arms covered in cuts and burn marks. David stood there, sizing me up. I had no idea what he was thinking.

"You the kid who wants Percs?" he finally asked.

"Yup."

David rummaged through his front hip pocket before handing over two small white pills. "Five bucks a pop, kid," he told me. "Does that sound okay?"

I bolted straight for my Honda, grabbed ten bucks from the console, and handed it to David. He put the two pills in my hand, and I swallowed them on the spot. By the time I got to Cate's later that night I was in high gear. The feeling of serenity I thought I had lost forever had finally returned.

A week later I pulled up at work, and as I was opening the door, suddenly there was David with his face pressed against the window. His eyes were popping out of his head, sweat was streaming down his face, and his breath was fogging up the window. It was almost ninety degrees out, but he was visibly shivering, and I could see that his pupils were dilated and fixed.

"Dude, what's up?" I asked him. "You don't look so good."

"My doctor just got busted," he told me. "My supply has dried up."

"Sorry, dude. That sucks," I replied.

I didn't give much thought to David's predicament. I liked David, but this was his deal. Besides, I figured another supplier would turn up. When you're using, you just learn to roll with the punches. I didn't know then that David was a full-blown addict and that he was going through withdrawal right in front of me.

"Dude, you have to know somebody who can get us some Percs," David pleaded with me.

"But I don't have a dope dealer," I tried to explain. "The only person who comes to mind is Brad."

David handed me his phone. "Jesse, call Brad now," he instructed. "Please."

I'd first met Brad in seventh grade, when we were in detention together all the time. Brad had an older brother named Jordan and a sister named Jessica. Jessica was much older than us. She married her high school sweetheart right after graduation and moved to Los Angeles. But Jordan and Brad were always in trouble, and I was often in trouble right along with them.

I called Brad. "Dude, I'm looking for some pain pills," I told him, but Brad didn't answer. Instead, he handed the phone to Jordan.

"I don't have Percocet, but I do have OxyContin," he told me.

"Never heard of it," I said.

"It's the strongest pain pill around," Jordan answered. "They give them to terminal cancer patients and shit."

I hung up and turned to David. "Dude, he doesn't have any Percs," I told him, and David stormed off, dejected.

That night I stood there watching David as he worked the line. He was sweating profusely, much more so than normal. Every couple of minutes he had to step away from his station to hurl. It was the first time I'd ever seen anyone dope-sick, experiencing the early withdrawal symptoms that are a way of life for an addict.

That Friday afternoon an impossibly long week at school and work finally ended. Cate and I were at my house. As usual, my mom was frantic as she hurriedly prepared for a long weekend at the Ritz-Carlton in South Beach with my parents' friends Arthur and Joanie. My parents loved their weekend trips to Palm Beach or Miami. Sometimes they went to Tampa to see my aunt Barbara and uncle George. A couple times a year my dad and my uncle Mark would drive up to Orlando for a big dental convention, and my mother would go away somewhere with her girlfriends.

Cate and I were lying on my bed. She tried to kiss me but could sense that I wasn't really there. Jordan's words about OxyContin were still ringing in my head.

Cate looked at me and asked, "Do we have enough weed for the weekend?"

"Probably not," I told her. "Let me call Brad and get an eighth."

As I hung up the phone I realized that I was out of money. I'd already burned through my paycheck. I walked into my parents' room and found my dad lying on the bed with the evening news on.

"Dad, I need some money," I told him.

"What's new, Jess?"

I told him some bullshit story about wanting to take Cate out to dinner and a movie. He handed me fifty bucks. "Make it last all weekend," he warned. I told Cate I'd be back and split for Brad's house. When I got there, the door was open. I bolted up the stairs and found Brad having a little gathering in his room. As usual, he was fogged out of his fucking mind. Everyone in the room was high from smoking weed and popping Ecstasy.

I got the weed I came for and then, as I walked down the hallway, I stopped by Jordan's room. His door was open just a crack, and he was talking on the phone. Jordan sounded congested, like he'd just woken up from a deep sleep. I looked at my watch. It was 4:00 P.M. I took a breath and walked into his room, knowing on some level that I was about to embark on a whole new path.

"Jesse, what the fuck do you want?" Jordan asked when he saw me.

"Dude, what's up with those pills you were talking about?"

Jordan sat up and told the person on the phone that he'd call them right back. He bent down and pulled what looked like a cigar box from under his bed. Slowly, he opened the box. Inside were dozens of small round blue pills and what looked like a pill cutter. "These are OC 80s," he told me. "Each one is the equivalent of sixteen Percocet." I started salivating, and my stomach turned with a combination of excitement and nervousness as Jordan took the pill cutter and cut a single pill into four equal parts. He handed me one quarter. "Take it and smoke a little pot," he instructed, and then added, "Enjoy the ride."

I handed Jordan ten bucks and bolted down the stairs to my car, full of what I can only describe as joy. Cate and I had the house to ourselves all weekend, the sun was shining, and I was holding a single piece of cellophane with a little slice of heaven inside. Sitting in my car, I blocked out the rest of the world. Nothing existed except for me and that little blue pill as I quickly swallowed it.

By the time I got back to my house I had already started to feel the warmth. It was like someone had draped a soft, warm blanket over my entire body. Nothing had ever made me feel that loved or cared for—not pot, not sex, not a compliment from my parents, not doing well at sports, and not even cooking gave me the same feeling of satisfaction. My parents had already left for the weekend. Cate and I snuggled up on the couch to watch the first two *Godfather* movies. Eight hours later, when we'd finished both movies, the Oxy was still kicking. I was in love.

I could still feel the effects of the Oxy the next morning. Right away I wanted more, but I didn't have any money to buy more. When I got my check the following weekend, I went straight to Jordan's to buy another quarter. This time I talked Cate into sharing it with me. She tried it and immediately vomited all over my patio. She could tell how strong it was, and it freaked her out. Cate had an inner restraint that I lacked, and she made me swear that I would never do Oxy again. But I knew I'd never be able to keep that promise.

Not long after, I met up with Jim on a Monday afternoon before work and told him about my experience with Oxy. Of course he was game to try it. We made a plan to meet at another restaurant in town called Beef 'O' Brady's. There each of us swallowed a quarter. Like it did with Cate, the Oxy made Jim vomit, but he loved the feeling as much as I did and wanted to do it again. He convinced me to make it a regular routine. Mondays quickly became OC Mondays. We both started with a quarter. Soon the quarter became a half, and then a half became three quarters, and before long three quarters became the whole pill. We went from swallowing to snorting, which made it hit us harder, faster, and therefore that much better. OC Mondays soon morphed into OC Tuesdays and Wednesdays and Thursdays and Fridays.

By the time I was seventeen I was physically addicted to OxyContin. Every morning I woke up feeling incredibly anxious and depressed. Nothing would help but OxyContin or Darvocet or some other opiate. My body needed the pills to function, just like a regular person needs food and water. Pills were my fuel.

As my junior year drew to close I completely lost interest in school and just stopped going. On the rare days when I did show up to school, I was popping pills like a madman—ten Percocets or fifteen Darvocets a day was pretty much the norm. I just nodded off in the back of class. No one knew what the hell was wrong with me. The other kids assumed I was stoned, but I was way beyond stoned.

My parents were too distracted by their own lives to notice, especially after my dad felt a lump in his groin and was later diagnosed with lymphoma. He kicked it into high gear, traveling around the country to get multiple opinions from every expert he could find before having it removed. This incident scared me, but I drowned that feeling with pills.

One day I approached my parents about dropping out of

high school. My argument was simple—I was attending culinary school by day and cooking at restaurants by night. By then I'd gotten really good and had been promoted to the front of the line at The Seawater Grill. For once I was honest with my parents about my intentions. "I don't want to go to high school," I told them. "I'm passionate about cooking, and I'm good at it. Why don't you just let me get a GED?" My parents gave me no resistance and were completely understanding about my decision. "Just be the best chef you can be, Jesse" was all my father said.

Once I dropped out of high school, I focused on cooking even more. At school I was studying "Baking and Pastry" with Chef Steve, learning how to make all sorts of quick breads, Danish, cakes, pies, and tarts. I never had much of a sweet tooth, but when I made puff pastry for the first time, laying down layer after layer of dough and getting my hands covered in grease in the process, I fell in love and gained a whole new appreciation for fresh baked goods.

Meanwhile, I felt that I'd learned just about everything I could from working at The Seawater Grill and was eager to move on. Jim was working at Graffiti and felt the same way. We talked to Chef Steve, who said we should be working at the best restaurant in the county, an award-winning café I'll call Smith's in Pompano Beach. Smith's was run by a well-respected celebrity chef. Jim went down there and got a job immediately. He was always ahead of the game, but I was younger and lived farther away. For my seventeenth birthday, I begged my parents to make a reservation at Smith's. I'd called numerous times, but the chef either wasn't there or didn't want to talk to me. This time, when we got there, Jim was in the back making salads, and he introduced me to the chef. He must have admired my persistence because he told me to show up for work the next day at three o'clock.

The job at Smith's paid only $7 an hour. It was less money than I was making at Seawater, but a step up on the career ladder.

I was put in charge of a dish called Cav Pie, one of Smith's signature dishes. It was basically a layer of sour cream covered with onions and four different colors of caviar. My job was to put the mixture into a mold so that it resembled a pie. Then I cut it into small wedges, put it on a plate with toast points, and passed it through the window to the grill cook. For the dinner shift, everyone would sit down at the same time and I'd quickly get slammed. But there was a fire inside of me to be the fastest, best cook they'd ever seen. I figured out little tricks that helped me go faster, like cutting the ends off the bread and putting it in the toaster ahead of time, so that when the order came through all I had to do was cut the bread. On my first night I was knocking out the Cav Pie so efficiently that the grill cook looked at me in awe and asked, "Damn, kid, are you pre-toasting the bread?" In less than six weeks I was up on the line cooking alongside him.

But as my addiction to OxyContin grew, my performance at work suffered. I started coming in late and leaving early, or showing up to work dope-sick on days when I couldn't get any pills. I started out strong at Smith's but eventually became the weak link as I started letting my addiction get in the way of my career.

Jim and I were doing some crazy shit. We were popping all sorts of pharmaceuticals—whatever we could find, really. If we couldn't get ahold of anything we wanted, sometimes we'd drive through the ghetto in Fort Lauderdale and pick up some cocaine. A handful of times we wound up getting crystal meth, instead, but had no idea until taking a bump and experiencing the worst burn imaginable shooting up into our brains. An hour later when our brief euphoria transformed into discombobulated pacing, we realized that this was not cocaine.

Sometimes we'd set each other up in the employee bathroom, setting lines of cocaine or OC up for each other under the toilet paper roll. Every night we made the same pledge that we weren't going to do it again the next day because we didn't want to get hooked, but inevitably by the end of the night we'd look at each other and say, "Fuck it." We had to score. We were a terrible influence on each other. Once we decided to get high, we'd call Jordan from the office phone at Smith's. "I'm going to sleep in twenty minutes," he'd tell us. "Be here by then." We knew he meant it. If we didn't get there in time, he'd lock the door and ignore the sound of us pounding on it. So we'd throw the phone down, change our clothes, and then speed to Jordan's house, weaving in and out of traffic just to get there in time. One time I was rushing so fast to get to Jordan's that I hit the median and cracked my fender. But that didn't bother me. I just kept driving.

CHAPTER FOUR

Pickle

Pickle: To preserve food by anaerobic fermentation in brine or vinegar. This procedure gives the resulting food, called a pickle, a salty or sour taste.

Going to culinary school in the morning and working at the restaurant at night left plenty of hours in the day for me to fill. I started spending more time with friends who shared what was at this point my main interest: pills. My buddy Fred got on the Oxy Train pretty fast. It didn't take much to get him to try what I considered a life-changing pill. Fred had a neighbor named Skyler who dabbled in some not-so-kosher shit. Skyler told us to check out a guy named Phil. We went through Fred's stepdad's change collection, filled a few socks with quarters, and took them to the change machine at Albertson's. Then we went to meet the dope dealer.

Phil worked at a jewelry store in Pompano Beach that was basically right down the street from Smith's. I went into the shop and asked for Phil. He immediately led me into a back room where customers weren't normally allowed. "You know Skyler?" he asked me.

"Yeah," I replied. "What do you have?"

Phil grabbed a backpack and dumped dozens of bags full of pills onto a table. He didn't have any Oxys, but there was more than enough Percocet, Darvocet, and Vicodin to keep Fred and me occupied for a while. I took whatever I could get with the money I had and went on my way.

Now that I had my GED, Fred and I started making plans to go on a three-week trip to Europe. I had been to Europe a few times with my family as a kid, but I'd never really traveled without them. Since neither of us was attending college, Fred and I saw this trip as our own warped version of a semester abroad. Our parents spoke to one another and came up with a plan. Fred's parents bought the Eurail passes, and my parents bought the plane tickets. My dad gave me a credit card for emergencies. At home my parents paid for everything. I didn't have to worry about things like rent, insurance, or paying for a car or gas. When I needed money for drugs, I milked my dad into giving me fifty or a hundred bucks. I supplemented this with the money I made working, but was still able to save quite a bit.

I took a few weeks off work, Fred and I scored a bunch of Oxys for the plane ride, and we were off. The trip to Europe came together within weeks of us voicing our desire to do it. We didn't have any plans other than working our way south so we would make it to Madrid three weeks later to catch a flight home. Until then, we were free, and we landed in London feeling like we owned Europe. We took the Chunnel to Holland, but by the time we arrived in Rotterdam we were already out of drugs and dope-sick. We figured Amsterdam would be the best place to score, so we made our way to the

city's infamous red light district. A dealer we met there offered to sell us heroin, but by the time he took off with our
money we realized he had ripped us off. Whatever we snorted
made us both sick and didn't even get us high. We sat at
Bulldog's Café for hours, smoking weed, drinking beer, and
strategizing how to score some pills.

Before taking that trip, I had never even considered paying for sex, but there was no way I wasn't going to take
advantage of Amsterdam's active (and legal) sex trade. Besides being dope-sick, Fred and I were both missing our
girlfriends—we needed something to distract us. And who
could resist the windows advertising a 50 GUILDER SUCK
AND FUCK? We walked around for maybe an hour and a half,
looking at all the prospects, before I finally settled on one
blond woman. She had a nice smile and gleaming white teeth
and was wearing an orange bikini. I walked over to the door.
"What's up?" I asked her.

"Fifty guilders for a suck and fuck," she replied with a
coy smile.

"Are you naked?"

"That's twenty-five extra," she told me.

I realized I'd better make sure I knew all the fine print,
so I started asking about positions. Finally I asked her,
"How about one hundred for everything?" She agreed, and I
thought I had covered all my bases, but once I got inside she
told me that the deal was only for twenty minutes. "That's
not good enough," I protested. "I need thirty minutes."

In response, the woman started laughing. "Everyone says
they want thirty minutes," she told me, "but they always
finish before fifteen." I took that as a challenge, but I ended

up losing twenty guilders because I was done in less than five.

Fred and I made our way to the South of France, stopping first in Paris and then moving on to St. Raphael, a beautiful coastal town on the Mediterranean. On the trains, we chain-smoked cigarettes and watched the graffiti pass us by. We could barely appreciate how beautiful St. Raphael was because we were so dope-sick and miserable, but I was able to appreciate the town's amazing food markets.

At all the restaurants I had worked at in Florida, we ordered what we needed from vendors and the food came already broken down. We never saw an actual butcher or even a whole animal. But at the French markets the butchers sold directly to the customers, and their products were incredible. I stopped at a butcher's stall and stared in awe at a simple chicken, amazed by how small and white it was. In America the chickens were huge and yellow because they were stuffed from a diet of corn, but in France they didn't manipulate the soil or the animals in any way. I moved on to a vegetable stand and without thinking reached out to touch a beautiful purple eggplant, but the farmer quickly slapped my hand away. He took so much pride in the produce his family grew that he insisted on handing the eggplant to me. This was the first time I really thought about sourcing ingredients and where the food I cooked with actually came from.

Despite our surroundings, Fred and I were having a hard time getting by without a steady supply of pills. One afternoon we sat on the beach, staring out into the turquoise water. Out of nowhere Fred jumped up and announced, "I need to sweat this shit out." He pointed to an enormous floating dock maybe a mile from the shore. "I'm going to swim to that dock," he told me. As I watched Fred start swimming I knew I didn't want to sweat it out with him. Instead, I became completely determined to do whatever I had to do to get us drugs.

I immediately left the beach and walked to the nearest pharmacy. I asked for the pharmacist and made up an elaborate story about losing my luggage and the pain medication that I desperately needed along with it. The pharmacist didn't speak much English, but she got the gist of what I was saying. "For narcotiques you need a doctor's prescription," she said, but that didn't deter me. "Where's the closest doctor?" I asked her, and she informed me that there was only one doctor in the whole town. She gave me his name, and I immediately went to his office, which was inside a quaint little house.

I lucked out—the doctor was willing to see me. Knowing this was my only shot, I put on the performance of my fucking life. I told the doctor that I had severe spinal problems and back pain and that my doctor back home had put me on morphine and OxyContin. The doctor tried to examine me, and every time he touched my back I screamed out in pain. I could've won an Oscar for that performance, and the doctor bought it. But they didn't have the pills I was talking about in Europe; they sold different drugs. The doctor finally wrote me a script for a medication that was basically the equivalent of Percocet. The best part was that he included three refills.

I grabbed the script and ran back to the beach. Fred was sitting on the floating dock in the middle of the Mediterranean. I started waving to him like a madman, shouting, "I fucking got it!" He swam back to shore, and we went straight to the pharmacy to fill the script. We each popped two of the pills and went to a local hamburger joint on the beach, waiting for our bellies to get warm. But these pills weren't what we were used to. They were a time-release formula that worked very differently. An hour went by and nothing happened. We didn't feel anything. Another hour passed and still nothing. At this point we both thought the pills were bogus. Then all of a sudden . . . *whazam!* At the exact same moment we both started to feel the telltale tickle. The warmth and the sensation of complete peace and serenity that came with it overtook us.

From that point on we were like two pigs in shit. For the next two weeks we carried the script with us from city to city and refilled it when the pills ran out. The funny thing is, though, we didn't want to refill it. For some reason, right after scoring we decided that we wanted to kick our habit. I guess having the safety net of the script made us feel confident enough to try. We didn't want to admit to each other (or to ourselves) that we were hooked, so we tried to deny it by waiting as long as we could take it to score.

By the time we got to our next stop, Rome, we were dopesick and miserable. When I had told the guys at work about my trip, one of them told me about an amazing underground restaurant in Rome that was full of locals. Fred and I went there our first night in Italy, looking to distract ourselves with a good meal. This place gave a new meaning to the term "family-run." The mother, father, and grandmother were all cooking in the kitchen while the kids ran around downstairs. None of them spoke any English, but it didn't matter. I ordered their specialty: Tripe Parmesan, which was fried pig stomach baked with a classic tomato sauce and homemade cheese. I ate every bite of the amazing meal along with delicious homemade bread dipped in good olive oil. But I was so dope-sick that as soon as I got the food down, it came back up and went all over the table. The family who owned the place started cursing at me in Italian. They quickly ran over and folded up the whole tablecloth with our used plates and my vomit inside, the whole time yelling at us to *uscita*— to "exit."

That was enough for me to give up on trying to kick the pills. I filled the script, and the rest of the trip was a drug-fueled orgy of food, booze, sex, and of course pills. Fred and I went from Rome to Florence, which was the city that had the biggest impact on me in terms of food. Fred and I met a group of South African girls there who took us out to small hole-in-the-wall places that tourists didn't know about. They always told the waiters that I was a chef so the restaurant's chef would come out and talk to us, but I wasn't really a chef. I was just a kid who wanted to be one. When the chefs came out, the girls translated for me, and I learned how passionate these chefs were about the ingredients they used and about making sure they were locally sourced.

One night we ordered a dish with veal head and the chef came out beforehand to show us the head. Then he proceeded to tell us in broken English all about the farm where it was raised, which had been run by his family's neighbor for several generations. He explained that because the chickens used the land first, their feces fertilized the soil. Then the veal ate that grass. We could have walked from the restaurant to the farm—that's how close it was—and the chef told me that he wouldn't use anything from more than ten or twelve kilometers away.

Another night the girls took us down a back alley in a quiet, residential neighborhood to a restaurant called Il Latini. Everything was dark and silent until we turned the corner and suddenly saw a guy holding a clipboard, calling out names, and forty or fifty people waiting to go inside. When we finally sat down, hanging overhead were dozens of hams that were sliced and thrown down on the table with fresh melon. We ate ribolita, a traditional Tuscan soup made with kale, savoy cabbage, leeks, carrots, celery, red onion, white beans, and tomato and thickened with whole wheat bread; wild boar cooked with tomatoes, red wine, and chocolate; and a delicious Florentine steak. I had never seen these simple, hearty dishes in the United States, but they were just part of a normal day in Florence. Through the debauchery I took all of this in and saved the menus from every restaurant I ate at.

On our last night in Florence, Fred and I went for a walk past the train station to the city's only McDonald's, which was a known hangout for hookers. We saw one girl who was tall and thin with dark, flawless skin, wearing a trench coat and nothing else. I took her back to the hotel, but I was so wasted that I couldn't come. She was servicing me in the bathtub while I looked at a porn magazine, but no matter what she did, there was no way it was going to happen. "I'm going to have to charge you double," she told me in disgust. Amazingly, this wasn't the last time I would hear that line. It's embarrassing but true—dope dick is real.

As soon as the girl left the hotel room we bolted for the train to Montpellier in the South of France, which was leaving in less than an hour. It was night, but we were too high to sleep on the eight-hour train ride. The time of day meant nothing to us on that trip. The hours blended into each other in a haze of drugs and sheer momentum. In Montpellier, we stumbled out of the nightclubs at four or five in the morning, when the bakers were just showing up to work and starting production. On the walk back to the hotel the streets were suffused with the sweet smell of fresh pastries.

One night in Montpellier we went to an American nightclub that was blasting Nirvana and had a Chevrolet coming out through the roof. We were already strung out on pills and immediately started throwing back tequila shots and smoking hash. After a while I couldn't stay awake any longer.

"Dude, I'm fucking done," I told Fred. "I'm going back to the room."

"Okay, I think I'll stay a little longer," he replied.

"Cool, bring back some chicks," I said, but I was mostly joking. I went to the hotel and passed out. The next thing I knew Fred was shaking me.

"Jesse, wake up!" I rubbed my eyes, put on my glasses, and looked up. Fred was standing at the foot of the bed surrounded by five women. None of them spoke any English, but they understood ménage à trois quite well.

The final stop on our trip, and also the wildest, was Barcelona. On the train ride there Fred and I started talking to two girls who were tall, blond, and gorgeous. They spoke perfect English and looked like two girls who had grown up in California, but they were actually from Sweden and told us they had studied Swedish massage. We gave them the name of the hotel we were staying at on Las Ramblas, the city's boisterous and downright sketchy main drag.

That night there was a knock at the door. Fred and I looked at each other in surprise before opening it. There stood our two Swedish friends. "We want to practice our technique," they told us.

After they left several debaucherous hours later, Fred and I decided to go for a walk. It was late, ten or eleven at least, but we were high and restless and the city was just starting to come to life. After getting hustled multiple times by some guys playing three-card monte on Las Ramblas, we arrived at a nightclub. As soon as we walked in a woman standing just inside the entrance asked, "Do you want Ecstasy?" We said yes, and she immediately grabbed me, pulled my body to hers, and started kissing me. Before I knew what was going on she slid a pill under my tongue and then did the same thing with Fred. After a few minutes we were gone, off together in some distant universe.

We stumbled out of the club hours later, still high, and walked to the end of Las Ramblas until we saw a marquee reading LIVE SEX SHOWS. We didn't know what this meant, but we had to check it out. A woman who had to be at least seventy-five years old checked our IDs, and after we paid she stamped our hands and pointed down a long, narrow flight of stairs. Finally we entered a big open room with a stage and a bunch of chairs. In the first row of chairs sat Japanese businessmen who were all holding cameras.

Fred and I sat down, having no idea what to expect. After a while a woman walked onto the stage and took off all her clothes, then got on all fours and started touching herself. We were only two feet from the stage and couldn't believe our eyes. The woman then came out into the crowd and started touching us, kissing my ear and playing with Fred's hair. Finally she stopped in front of one guy and started dragging him up onto the stage. At first he protested, but it was obvious that he was part of the act. He eventually went up onstage, and the woman started blowing him right there in front of us. The Japanese guys seemed totally into it, but Fred and I were pretty freaked out. After a few minutes the two of them started fucking, and when he finished, everybody started clapping on cue as if they were watching a performance of *West Side Story*.

The whole time this was going on women started coming around and trying to seduce the men in the audience. One woman came up to me who had to weigh at least 250 pounds. She looked like a linebacker for the Jets. I was getting turned on from watching what was going on onstage, but I didn't really want to have sex with her. "I just want a blow job," I told her. The woman grabbed me, threw me over her shoulder, and carried me off. She threw me into a chair and started pulling my dick out of my pants. Suddenly the old woman who had checked us in was standing in front of me, shining a flashlight in my face. "Give me the money," she yelled. I handed it over, and she left the other woman to her job. Suffice it to say, it was worth every penny.

The rest of our time in Barcelona was spent tapas hopping along Las Ramblas, indulging in local beers and delicious seafood—mussels and anchovies that had, amazingly, come out of a can. I had grown up believing that any food from a can was automatically gross, but in Barcelona it was completely different; this was high-quality stuff, drowning in the best Spanish olive oil.

By the time we arrived in Madrid for our flight home, we had run through the last of our refills of the pills and were dope-sick again. Having no idea how we'd survive the eight-hour flight home without getting straight, I was determined to score. We went to the pharmacy in the airport, and I told them the same story I had concocted in France, including the fact that I couldn't fly without my pain pills and I was afraid I'd have a panic attack. The pharmacist again told me I needed a script, so I pleaded, "How can I talk to a doctor?" She got a doctor on the phone and handed it to me, and I somehow convinced the doctor over the phone to write me a script for five Vicodin—just enough to last the flight.

Fred couldn't believe I had managed to convince a doctor to write a prescription for me over the phone, and I couldn't really believe it either. But when I needed to score, I always found a way. Fred and I walked to the gate, and a few minutes later we heard them calling my name. The pharmacy had sent my prescription to the gate on a go-cart so that I wouldn't miss my flight. Fred and I immediately each took half of the pills, passed out, and woke up eight hours later in the States.

As soon as I got home everyone could tell that I was different. I went back to work at Smith's, but my motivation was gone. My addiction was at a new level. Cate knew I had cheated on her in Europe. She sensed the change in me, and we quickly broke up. It's possible that I was looking for an excuse, but I saw this as just another reason to continue going downhill.

CHAPTER FIVE

Consommé

Consommé: A clear soup made from bouillon or stock with a mixture of ground meats, carrots, celery, onions, tomatoes, and egg whites. Simmering the consommé for a long time while frequently stirring it brings impurities to the surface of the liquid, which are further drawn out by the presence of acid from the tomatoes.

Back from Europe, I was seventeen years old with a GED, no ambition for any more school, and a raging drug habit. My friends were heading to other cities and states to start college, and I felt stuck at home and restless. My friend Charnam was starting his freshman year at Florida State University in Tallahassee, and I convinced my parents that I should go up there with him. I told them I would room with Charnam, enroll at a community college, and get a job. They went right along with this plan, even helping me move in and buying me everything I needed for my new apartment.

Two days after arriving in Tallahassee I was out of drugs and dope-sick. I needed to score. Thinking I could replicate my amazing luck in Europe, I started scouring the phone book and calling up area hospitals. Finally, one of the operators pointed me in the direction of a methadone clinic. By the time I called it was already closed for the day. "Come down tomorrow, honey," the clinic's receptionist told me.

First thing the next morning I drove about fifteen minutes to the clinic, which was located in a grim, partially deserted strip mall. It was starting to dawn on me how different Tallahassee was from South Florida. It was like the Deep South, and decal-laden pickup trucks filled the parking lot that morning. Outside, a group of people huddled together, nervously swaying from foot to foot while smoking an endless succession of cigarettes. Inside, the common area smelled of stale smoke. An old television was turned on to the news, and a dry-erase board listed everyone's name and how long they had been clean.

When it was my turn to meet with the doctor, he performed a cursory physical. This time I didn't have to put on much of an act. I hadn't been shooting drugs, but after checking my pulse and my pupils, the doctor could see that I was indeed going through withdrawal. I was approved immediately and made my way over to the nurses' station. "Bless you, child," a nurse named Maryann greeted me. Short, chubby, and covered in freckles, she was wearing colorful nurse's scrubs. Behind Maryann was a large container shaped like a fish tank and filled with a pink liquid. New patients started with fifteen milligrams a day, going up or down five milligrams until they reached the right dose. "That will be eleven dollars, Mr. Schenker," Maryann said. I handed her the money and got my dose.

Back in my car, Tool was playing on the radio and I felt great. For just eleven bucks a day I could get legally loaded. The only catch was that I had to be at the clinic by 9:00 A.M.

every morning, but I was ecstatic to have stumbled upon this place. Every day I went up five milligrams until I got to fifty or sixty milligrams. But I wasn't doing anything else. I had signed up for classes at the community college, but after attending maybe three classes I just stopped going. My parents were paying for everything, so I had no motivation to look for a job.

Instead, I just sat alone in my apartment eating candy bars and smoking cigarettes. The methadone clinic was the only place I went other than the supermarket. Being fucked up on methadone severely affected my most basic bodily functions. I stood over the toilet for fifteen minutes waiting for urine to come out. But I still cooked. One night I woke up in the middle of the night and started making doughnuts from scratch in my underwear. Another time I went to the supermarket, bought a duck, and proceeded to make a seven-course tasting menu for Charnam and some friends at 3:00 A.M.

It didn't take long for me to become hooked on methadone. I knew I was drifting, and it bothered me that I was becoming a hermit. In Parkland I had always felt like an outsider but had been able to connect with friends who were misfits like me. Tallahassee was different, and I quickly learned it was more populated with blue-collar workers than the privileged world I'd grown up in. I was so used to my parents satisfying my every need, I had no idea how to live in the real world. These people woke up every day not knowing what sort of pain they would face or where their next meal would come from, and instead of feeling grateful to my parents for sparing me this, I resented the fact that I'd never learned how to fend for myself.

Despite how determined I was to become more independent, even I could see that there was nothing for me in Tallahassee. I could tell it was a dead end, and after only a few months there I went back to Parkland. I moved back in with my parents and returned to my job at Smith's as if nothing had changed, except for my new addiction to methadone.

When I told them I was leaving, the clinic in Tallahassee made arrangements in advance for me to transfer to a new methadone clinic in Pompano. Compared to Tallahassee, this clinic was busier and brought in a different world. While three-quarters of the patients were the same types of junkies I'd seen at the other clinic, there was also a small percentage of functioning addicts. I lined up every morning alongside doctors, lawyers, businessmen, and soccer moms as we waited with the other junkies to get our shots.

Other than methadone, drugs had been hard to come by in Tallahassee, but that wasn't a problem in Broward County. Back home, I fell back in with my same group of friends, and within weeks my pill addiction resurfaced with a vengeance. At the new methadone clinic there were "therapists" whose job it was to monitor the patients and make sure they weren't using. Sometimes they pulled someone out of line and interrogated him or her with a bunch of questions. Other times they selected someone for random drug testing. In the back of my head I knew my luck was running out, but that didn't stop me from using. Most days I showed up to the clinic either loaded or dope-sick.

Sure enough, on Monday, January 20, I received my last dose of methadone. The next day the clinic booted me out for pissing dirty. For weeks they had been pumping me full of the strongest opiate imaginable, and because I dabbled on the side I was booted out. Suddenly I was without a daily source of opiates. Heroin gets all the notoriety when it comes to withdrawal, but kicking methadone is actually much worse. Heroin and methadone have similar withdrawal characteristics, but methadone takes it to a deeper level. At first I just started feeling jittery. Then came prolonged and very painful muscle spasms. My whole body felt like a rubber band being pulled taut one minute and contracting the next. The pain was unbearable. I felt it deep in my bones and slowly, inexorably rising through my body, penetrating every pore and fiber. Within hours I was writhing on the floor, screaming at the top of my lungs.

I couldn't deal with it. I needed relief. A friend told me about a place where all of the junkies went, a hole-in-the-wall pain clinic housed in a Coral Springs strip mall. I drove right over and pulled into a nearly vacant parking lot. The dingy strip mall contained five storefronts, two of which were vacant. Situated between a laundromat and a deli was a large door with peeling gray paint. Inside was a small vestibule, much like in any other doctor's office, but there was no receptionist waiting behind the glass. There were five ratty chairs crammed into a closet-sized waiting area and two extra folding chairs against the wall outside the doctor's office.

It was just past 9:00 A.M., and already the place was packed. One after another, people walked in—construction workers, domestics, crack whores, trailer trash—a cadre of cash-strapped misfits looking to get fixed. I pulled up a chair and waited. Only a minute later the door opened and a tall man with deep-set brown eyes and curly gray hair walked into the waiting room. "Next," he announced without looking up.

It was strictly first come first served, and when my turn came I entered the doctor's office to find no examination table, no patient chart, no stethoscope, and no sink. There was just a small brown desk stacked high with papers and a safe tucked into one corner. I sat down and started making small talk with the doctor. "My parents have the same kind of dog," I said, looking at a picture of the doctor and his Maltese sitting on his desk. I had named my parents' first Maltese Cutie Pie when I was five years old.

"What's a nice Jewish kid like you doing here?" the doctor asked me in response, ignoring my comment about the dog.

"Same as everyone else, I guess."

"You don't belong here," he told me. "You know that."

I disagreed. I had little money and was dope-sick, so I belonged there as much as anyone else. In my heart, I knew that I was no better than the junkies who filled the waiting room.

"Five dollars," he told me, and I handed him the money. "Roll up your sleeve." He wiped my arm with an alcohol pad and gave me a shot of Buprenex, a narcotic analgesic, right in my bicep. I went back into the waiting room. Fifteen minutes later I didn't feel high, but the agony had receded. At least that was something.

I quickly became a regular at the pain clinic. Anytime I was short of cash and needed to get straight, I went there. It was junkie central, a great place to make connections and learn new tricks. Before long I was going every day. Even the unflappable doctor seemed concerned. "Jesse, opiates affect your liver," he told me, writing something down on a prescription pad. "Take some milk thistle." He ripped off the sheet and handed it to me.

A couple of days later my dad approached me holding the doctor's note. "Milk thistle," he said, sounding bewildered. "What the fuck is this all about?"

"I went to a doctor," I told him calmly. "Something with my liver, but it's nothing. Don't worry about it." I tried to wave it off.

My dad has always been a pretty big hypochondriac, and now his radar was lit up. He started checking on me, coming into my room in the middle of the night to find me shaking and sweating. His denial about my drug use was so strong that he started to believe I was suffering from an unrelated medical issue.

The pain clinic fueled my addiction, but the doctor wouldn't give me more than a certain amount. He couldn't have his patients dropping dead on him, so he carefully walked the line. But I needed more. My addiction was so bad that I would be dope-sick just a few hours after leaving the clinic. There was no way the doctor would keep up with my body's demands. I remembered Phil at the jewelry store with his ample supply of pills. I hadn't seen Phil in months, not since I left for Tallahassee, but I called him up anyway. "I need some OCs," I told him.

"Meet me in the back of the shop," he said, but this time he didn't have a backpack full of drugs. "I don't have any shit on me," he told me. "I'm doing things a little different now. Give me your number and I'll have my guy call you." Maybe I should have recognized this as a red flag, but I was too desperate to care.

The next day I got a call on my cell from an unknown number. I answered right away, knowing it must be Phil's guy, and heard a gravelly voice ask, "Is this Jesse?"

"Yeah," I said. "Who's this?"

"This is Poncho, Phil's boy," he said. "You looking for Oxys? I can hook you up, no problem."

We agreed to meet the next day at a rest stop on the Sawgrass Expressway. It was the perfect place to meet, full of drug dealers, hustlers, teenage boozehounds, truckers, and tired drivers looking for a breather. There were cops around, but the Florida Highway Patrol, which scouted highway rest areas, was always complaining about shortages, so I figured we were cool. I found Poncho right away. Short and fat with a long scraggly beard and a large, hair-covered mole on his cheek, he fit the role of a dealer perfectly. I got into his run-down El Camino.

"What are you looking for?" he asked me. "Phil tells me you're looking to go big."

I wanted a steady supply of pills just for my own consumption, but I didn't want to tell him that, so I concocted some bullshit story. "I'm well funded," I said. "I got a guy who's looking for a steady line of Oxy."

"I can get you 150 in a couple of days," he said. "Let's start small. Get five hundred cash and I'll call you in forty-eight."

A couple of days later it was just an hour before dinner service was going to start up at Smith's. The restaurant was booked solid, and I knew it was going to be a madhouse. As

I set up my station I wasn't feeling good at all. I was sweaty and shaky as I started peeling some beets. Then I felt the phone vibrate in my pocket. I scrambled out back, smearing my cheek with bright red beet juice as I rushed out the door.

"You got the money?" Poncho asked.

"Yeah," I told him. "You got the pills?"

"I'll be out back in a minute," he said. "Meet me there."

I grabbed the cash and hopped into Poncho's car. He drove up the block a bit before pulling into an empty parking lot. "Show me the money," he instructed. I reached into my pocket, pulled out five $100 bills, and handed them to him. He dumped the pills in the center console, and just as I was reaching for the pills the car door opened.

"Don't you move, motherfucker!" That would have been hard to do. I'd just been yanked out of the passenger seat and thrown onto a narrow stretch of sunbaked pavement. My right cheek was pressed firmly into the ground, and blood oozed from my nose and chin as my hands were cuffed behind my back. The heel of a boot was wedged into the middle of my spine. I couldn't move a muscle. To top it all off, I was dope-sick. It had been hours since I last scored; I needed those pills from Poncho.

Then I heard the guns click. "Where are the fucking drugs?"

"I don't have any," I said into the ground. "I'm not a fucking drug dealer." It didn't matter that for once I was telling the truth. Five big, burly cops lifted me off the ground and leaned me against the back of a large, unmarked SUV with tinted windows. Their jackets read DEA and BROWARD SHER-IFF'S OFFICE, and they were holding shotguns, all pointed in my direction, as they arrested me for trafficking OxyContin. Phil had set me up. I didn't know it at the time, but he had been busted while I was living in Tallahassee and became a narc for the police to avoid some major fucking prison time.

With cops on either side of me, I climbed into the backseat of the SUV. They drove me, not to jail, but to my parents' house. I was only seventeen, still a minor. I got out and walked up the driveway, still flanked by cops on either side. One of the cops walked over to the garage door and started banging. My dad walked out almost immediately, wearing shorts and a Bob Dylan T-shirt. His hair was slightly disheveled, as if he had just woken up from a nap. He took off his glasses and rubbed his eyes before looking in my direction.

"We've arrested your son for trafficking OxyContin," the cop informed my dad. "It's a serious charge." My dad started moving toward me with blood in his eyes. For a minute I thought he was going to kill me, but the cops restrained him. "Mr. Schenker, we need your permission to search the premises," the cop said, and my dad helplessly motioned for them to enter. The cops rummaged through my room, but it was a perfunctory search. It didn't take them long to realize I was an addict, not a dealer. But that didn't stop them from taking me to jail.

By the time my parents bailed me out the next day I had already started detoxing. The car ride home was miserable. "What the fuck are you doing trafficking OxyContin?" my dad wanted to know. For once, I didn't have a good answer. I was too sick and didn't even have the strength to come up with a cover story. When we got back to the house, my parents went into their room and closed the door without saying a word. Slowly, I walked over and placed my ear against the door. I heard them talking, my mother crying. It was nothing I hadn't heard before. More important to me in that moment was my need to get straight. My dad kept a money clip in a dish on the kitchen counter. Every day after work, without fail, he dropped the clip in that dish. I quickly walked over and lifted forty bucks. Minutes later my dad walked out of the bedroom. "I made an appointment for the three of us with Alan this afternoon," he told me, and then he walked out the door.

After he was gone, I approached my mother. Her face was drawn, her eyes red and puffy from crying. She grabbed a tissue and wiped her nose. Her vulnerability was palpable, and I swooped in like a falcon. "Mom," I said, "I'm going out for a pack of cigarettes."

"Jesse, I don't trust you," she said tearfully. "I don't want you to leave."

"It's just for cigarettes," I told her. "I'll be back in thirty minutes."

I called Jordan as I was walking out the door. "I need Oxy," I told him. "Can I meet you?"

"I'm leaving for work soon," he said. "Meet me in twenty minutes." I drove as fast as I could to his house.

That afternoon I sat down with Alan and my parents. The dope-sickness was gone, and I had steadied myself for what was coming. Alan had been warning my parents about my addiction for years, but now he was truly pissed. Drug trafficking was no slap on the wrist: I was being charged with a felony. "Jesse, you need rehab. This is serious," he said.

My dad made some calls the next day. A family friend

recommended a top-shelf criminal defense attorney who demanded a $15,000 retainer. My parents sat me down with the attorney a few days later. "Jesse," the attorney said, "you're in a lot of trouble. Drug trafficking is a fifteen-year mandatory minimum sentence." The attorney paused for a moment, and then said, "Just get yourself clean, fix your life, and we'll work something out."

The attorney advised my parents to use a twenty-eight-day provision in my insurance policy to get me into drug and alcohol rehab at Fort Lauderdale Hospital. He explained that this might help me avoid spending time in prison. Beyond the legal ramifications, putting me in rehab also helped ease my parents' fears. They were overwhelmed and scared, with no clue what to do with me. But twenty-eight days was a drop in the bucket for someone like me who had been strung out for years. Those types of treatment programs are like a big revolving door for junkies. People bounce in and out, often doing better for a while and then relapsing. Others just give up and die. Not me. I didn't want to stop using. I didn't even think I had a problem.

After leaving the hospital, I went to Challenges Addiction Treatment Center. My parents told me this was my one shot at rehab. At Challenges we lived in residential housing and were transported by van to attend counseling sessions and recovery meetings and to run regular errands. It took me a week to figure out how to smuggle in drugs. We each received a $100 weekly food allowance (mine was supplied by my parents); I promptly used most of it to buy Oxy. This wasn't always easy. Dealers took advantage of my situation, and I had to pay double for home delivery, plus we were checked on every hour. But I got the timing down to an exact science with the same focus I had once used at Smith's to efficiently knock out the Cav Pie. When the counselors picked us up in a van once a week and took us to Publix to buy groceries, I'd have only a few dollars left. So I'd buy a few things and then flirt with the counselor or cause some other distraction to keep them from checking my bags to see how little I'd bought.

The problem with this plan was that I needed to eat, so I happily traded my skills in the kitchen. I started by lying to my roommate and telling him that my parents hadn't given me any money for groceries that week. Then I said, "Hey, I saw that you bought some chicken. Do you want me to make you a really nice roast chicken for dinner?" I cooked the dinner, and then of course he asked me to eat with him. Then, the next day in front of everyone, I asked him, "Hey, man, how was that roast chicken?" When everyone else heard him rave about my cooking, they asked me to cook for them too. Before long I always had someone to cook for—and eat with—and the money I needed to buy drugs.

The meals I cooked for the other patients were usually simple and nostalgic. While they were getting clean, they wanted to eat what their mothers had made for them growing up, so I cooked meatloaf with mashed potatoes, macaroni and cheese, and fried chicken. It wasn't about being creative or inventive then. Cooking was simply a tool I used to survive. My old buddy Sam was the only friend from home who stuck by me. When I was on furlough, he came to visit me, brought me groceries, and took me out to the movies.

Of course, we were subject to random drug testing at

Challenges, and this indeed provided a challenge. But somehow I lucked out. Those early tests didn't detect OCs. This was before the OxyContin epidemic really took hold, and because they are semisynthetic, OCs were untraceable by earlier urine testing. By month four at Challenges I qualified for work release and got my car back. I wasn't the only one who was still using while in rehab. One night at 10:00 my roommate asked me if he could borrow my car so he could drive to Miami to score. I said yes, adding, "If you're not back in three hours, I'm going to report the car stolen." When 4:00 A.M. rolled around and he was still nowhere in sight, I stayed true to my word. I found a groundskeeper and told him that my car had been stolen. About an hour later my roommate had been dropped off by the police. The car was wrecked. Apparently they couldn't wait to get high, so they shot up while driving and drove headfirst into a palm tree. I stuck to my story that he'd taken the car without my permission, and my insurance ended up covering the cost.

By month six, I graduated from Challenges and moved on to Incentives, a halfway house in Boca Raton. It was run by a couple of guys who were former heroin addicts from New York. They had relocated to Florida for their recovery and were both twenty-five years sober. Those hard-core guys would have done anything to help me get clean. At Incentives, everyone had to work, and I landed a sweet gig at a happening new Asian fusion restaurant in Boca Raton. I was responsible for the pasta station, cooking modern variations of classic pasta dishes with an Asian flare.

One of our signature pastas was Lobster Bolognese. Instead of the tomato sauce, spaghetti, and ground beef in a traditional Bolognese, I made lobster bisque with red chilies and Korean pepper flakes and served it with potato gnocchi and a whole Maine lobster. Right away I was back into it, getting to work early to cut the carrots, onions, and celery for the bisque and take apart the lobsters, preserving each claw so that it would look pretty perched on top of the dish. Another dish I loved to cook was a Thai pancake made of equal parts coconut milk and rice flour, whisked together into a batterlike consistency. I cooked the pancakes in small cast-iron pans, folded them up like tacos, and then stuffed them with rock shrimp and bean sprouts.

At this time a lot of chefs were bringing ingredients from Southeast Asia into the States, turning Asian fusion cooking into a big trend, but even before the culinary world was saturated with this style of cooking I enjoyed learning how to use classic techniques with new ingredients. I heated up sesame oil until it was smoking and then poured it over a piece of raw fish, loving the sound of the sizzle when the hot oil hit the fish.

But as much as I enjoyed working at the restaurant, I also wanted to get high. Soon I found a way to smuggle in OCs through my old coworker Dan. Once I had the job I moved out of the halfway house and managed to convince my parents to rent me an apartment. "I'm doing really good, and I've got a job," I told them. They were so relieved that I was clean (or so they thought) that they rented me a nice apartment on Verde Trail in Boca.

At the new restaurant I hooked up with a guy named Ya-Ya who was a badass cook. We worked the line together, but he ran fucking circles around me. He was like an acrobat, grabbing hot sizzle trays with his bare hands and using his fingertips to flip over softshell crabs that had been cooking at 350 degrees in the deep fryer. Ya-Ya topped off his culinary gymnastics with a profitable side business dealing cocaine. It didn't take long for him to persuade me to give it a try.

One night when I knew everyone else had left work I went into the restaurant's bathroom and dumped out some of the coke, using my driver's license to form a single straight line. I rolled up a dollar-bill and put one end in my left nostril. Using my right index finger, I closed my right nostril and snorted in as hard as I could. Almost immediately, my nose and throat went numb. It was well past 2:00 A.M. when I left the restaurant, but I felt full of energy. Soon I had a new schedule of getting by on blow during the week and looking forward to weekends with my OCs.

It didn't take long for me to need more, though. A little bit of coke during the week just wasn't cutting it. One day at work I was dope-sick. My pupils were dilated, and I felt nauseous. Every few minutes I had to run to the bathroom. I noticed Doug, the sous chef, watching me, and thought I was about to get in trouble for using on the job, but instead Doug approached me when I was in the walk-in gathering vegetables. He closed the door behind us and handed me a needle and a small bag of heroin. "You know what to do, right?" he asked.

"Of course," I said.

"Okay, you owe me," he said. "Get straight so you can get your ass back to work."

I had never shot drugs before. The Buprenex I'd gotten at the pain clinic was injected intramuscularly, not into the vein. Heroin was a whole new experience. I went into the bathroom and found an empty stall. I put the heroin in the same spoon I used to baste fish and mixed it with water. Putting the lighter to the bottom, I let it simmer for just a second. Then I tore a piece of cotton from a cigarette and threw it in the spoon. Mesmerized, I watched the cotton absorb the speckled brown liquid before I placed the needle in the spoon and carefully drew the liquid into the syringe, making sure to remove any lingering air bubbles. I rolled up the left sleeve of my chef's coat. There was no need for a tourniquet; I had veins that would give any junkie a wet dream. I jabbed the needle into my forearm, watching the blood snake into the syringe.

Pushing the plunger into that single vein was perhaps the most gratifying experience of my entire life to that point. In an instant, my whole body softened; years' worth of tension lifted right off me. From then on, I alternated. Some days I did heroin, and on other days I stuck to OCs. But there was no doubt about it. The worm had turned. There was no going back from here.

CHAPTER SIX

Ballotine

Ballotine: A boned chicken or duck thigh, stuffed with ground meat and other ingredients, that can be shaped like a sausage or re-formed to look like the leg, often with a clean piece of bone left in the end. Tied together to hold its shape and sometimes stitched up with a trussing needle, a ballotine is cooked by roasting, braising, or poaching.

Soon I was shooting up every day, but I still didn't really know the ins and outs of intravenous drug use. No one had handed me a manual to consult. I had to learn as I went. Doug gave me some pointers. "Save your cottons," he told me. "When you run short on dope, you can rinse the cottons and squeeze out the last little bit of drug." From then on, I stored my cottons in an old cigar box that I kept on my night table. When needed, I loaded them into the barrel of a syringe, drew in water, and squeezed until they were dry. I squirted the contents onto a spoon and used a new cotton to draw the smack into a syringe.

But one thing Doug never warned me about was cotton fever. Sometimes cotton fibers break off from the filter, and if they're dirty or carrying some bacteria that makes it into your bloodstream, you're fucked. Most addicts don't make it a point to carry sterile cotton balls or Q-tips. A clean filtered cigarette can do the trick, but most of the time you have to find a cigarette butt on the ground, in an ashtray, or from the garbage, which I did all the time.

I got my first taste of cotton fever one night about thirty minutes after shooting up. It whacked me upside the fucking head like I was on day two of the world's worst flu. My ears started ringing, and I felt a vicelike pressure on each side of my head. Sweat started oozing out of my every pore, and I began shaking uncontrollably. Then came bone-numbing chills as my temperature spiked to 105 degrees. I filled my bathtub with scalding hot water to try to warm up, but nothing helped. I just started shaking violently and vomiting nonstop. Thankfully, after a few hours it simply passed.

In time, heroin took over everything. Most days I couldn't even make it into work. I spent my days dope-sick, trying my best to cope. When I did show up, I was late and had track marks on my arms. "I have to do this, Jesse. You're a fucking mess," Doug said when he fired me. Pretty ironic, I thought, since he was the one who had introduced me to the stuff.

The worst part was having to tell my dad I'd been fired. "What's the matter with you, Jesse?" he asked.

Feeling like I was out of options, I confessed. "I'm using again," I told him.

My dad immediately kicked into high gear. "We're going to look after you here," he said. "We'll monitor you, take you to meetings." My dad has always been a problem solver, a take-charge kind of guy. He figured he could just detox me at home, but he didn't have any clue about the depth of the addiction I was dealing with.

My dad called a doctor friend and got me a prescription for Percocet. Then he and my mom took me to a new therapist, Larry Kreisberg. Larry had a much harder edge than Alan and didn't take any bullshit. During our first session Larry figured out that I was shooting drugs and got straight to the point: he demanded that I confront my parents. "You've got to tell them the truth," he said. Then he told me that I was going to be drug-tested at home just like I would be at a halfway house or in rehab.

During the car ride home I told my parents that I was shooting drugs. When we got home, they cried, hugged, and said that they couldn't believe this was happening. But the evidence was all there. My arms were littered with track marks. When they moved me out of my apartment in Boca, they'd seen how filthy and roach-infested it was. Now they finally realized this was a serious problem, and they were determined to help me fix it. They kept me under their thumb more than ever before.

At my parents' house I had no job, no money, and a raging drug habit. I had to get creative in order to score. I asked my dad to drive me to a meeting, walked in while he watched me from the car, and then took off to meet a dealer after he'd driven off. After a few weeks I convinced my parents to let me drive myself to meetings. This gave me an hour to score and get back to the house. But my dad wouldn't let me get a job, and I needed money. Little by little, I started taking our musical equipment to the pawnshop, eventually pawning my drum set and my dad's guitars, amplifiers, and stereos.

I found new dealers who met me at the Cypress Head gates to exchange money for drugs. One of those dealers, Trevor, was totally wild. He had done some serious prison time for driving under the influence and carrying a concealed weapon, but he always seemed to have a steady supply of OC. I learned how to shoot OCs by taking the blue pill and sucking off the time-release coating, leaving just the white pill. Then I carefully removed the cellophane wrapper from the bottom of a cigarette pack, dropped the pill into the cellophane, and took the bottom of a lighter to crush the pill until it was the texture of smooth powder. I placed the powder into a spoon and cooked it until it bubbled and there was a faint trace of steam above the spoon. I pushed the plunger down. Quickly, I became an expert. I could even drive a stick shift with one hand and fix with the other.

While this going on, Larry was counseling my parents on how to deal with me. He encouraged them to join Al-Anon and told them that they needed to cut me off at the knees. They had to stop enabling me, he told them. I needed to feel discomfort to make changes. But I knew my parents couldn't bear the thought of me experiencing discomfort, so I never believed they would follow Larry's advice.

When my parents went out for the night, I ransacked their closets. I found wads of cash in a shoebox. In my mom's closet I found gold chains from the '80s that she didn't wear anymore, pearls, and antique silverware. It was a treasure trove. I should have felt guilty, but I was addicted. I needed to get high every day, and it required a steady supply of cash. My conscience had evaporated.

There was one item I'd been eyeing for some time. It was a

watch with a beautiful oyster case milled from a single piece of metal, a gleaming eighteen-karat yellow gold exterior, and a diamond-studded dial. I knew that watch was worth a lot; $25,000 was the number I had heard tossed around. A watch like that could easily fetch a couple hundred bucks at a pawnshop, but grabbing it was a slight problem. My mother kept her daily jewelry in a bathroom drawer. I normally didn't go into that drawer. I went for the stuff she didn't wear, like diamond necklaces and big gaudy rings. She kept those in a large Ziploc bag in my dad's closet.

I was on my way out to meet Trevor when I heard my mother say it. "I can't find my Rolex. I think I must've misplaced it."

My dad didn't flinch. The words just tumbled out. "I think Jesse took it."

"No," my mother said. "It's around. I know it'll turn up."

My mother was still deep in denial, but my dad knew better. Over the years he was always the one to post bail, find an attorney, sign a lease, get me into rehab, and grease the wheel. Ever since I returned from Tallahassee, he had been watching me like a hawk. He saw that my skin was warm and flushed. At night he sat by my bed watching me toss and turn in my sleep. I was decomposing in front of my father's eyes, and there was nothing he could do to stop it.

I went into my parents' room, where my dad was lying on the bed. "Dad, can I borrow your car?" I asked. "I'm going to a meeting."

He didn't move an inch, but I'll never forget what he said. "Jesse, in my heart I could never throw you out," he told me. "But in my head I can and I will. Don't fuck with me. I want you back here in an hour and a half."

I grabbed the keys and sped off in my dad's Infiniti to meet Trevor. I had $500 cash in my pocket—not exactly a fair exchange for a $25,000 Rolex, but it was enough to score me two days' worth of OC. By then I was shooting 160 milligrams every few hours, enough to kill a small elephant.

While I was gone, my dad went into my room. It was a disaster area, but he rummaged through my stuff until he found what he was looking for. I was still driving when the phone rang. "Get the fuck home now," was all he said. For once, I didn't argue. I turned around and sped home. When I entered the kitchen from the garage, my dad was waiting for me at the table. "Jesse, what the fuck is this?" He was holding the receipt from the pawnshop.

I didn't have an answer, so I turned indignant. "What are you doing in my fucking room?" I desperately needed to turn the situation to my advantage, but for once, I couldn't. On that day there was no manipulating my father as he came face-to-face with the true extent of my addiction. So I turned up the volume, kicking over furniture and screaming at the top of my lungs. I could feel the veins in my temple bulging, every muscle in my body tense with rage. My dad was shocked. He had never seen that side of me before. For years I had been playing the role of the docile manipulator. I'd acted out with my actions, but never before with words.

"Drugs or family," my father said with an eerie calm in his voice. "You can't have both, Jesse." I looked him in the eye, and in an instant I knew I had to go. I couldn't remain in my parents' house for another minute. I quickly threw some things in a bag and walked out. My father was standing in the driveway. "Let me take you to Broward General," he offered, but I just ignored him and kept walking until I got to the clubhouse, where I called my friend Luisa. "Come pick me up. I have some cash. I need to get out of here."

The next few weeks were a blur of drugs and debauchery as I bounced from one home of an oddball junkie who agreed to take me in to the next. It never lasted long; my stash would be gone almost immediately, and once my hosts realized that I didn't have any drugs or money, they'd give me the boot. All I had were the clothes I'd stuffed in my backpack. To find me, my friends drove around looking for me because I didn't even have a phone. One day Sam tracked me down and told me, "I got your stuff back," with an angry bite to his voice. "The pawnshop didn't argue with me when I told them they'd bought it from a heroin junkie. What's the matter with you, Jesse? There was so much shit there I couldn't fit it all in the back of my car."

I knew Sam was trying to scare me straight, and I was honestly a little bit afraid of him. Sam wasn't like me. Sure, we had gotten in trouble together when we were kids, but he'd grown up and was living a normal life by then. I still couldn't imagine such a thing for myself. Sam brought me back to his place and even took a few days off work to look after me while I detoxed on his couch. He fed me spoonfuls of cough syrup with codeine to take the edge off, but other than that, he made it clear that he would not accept any dalliances. One day I walked into his bedroom and found him sitting on the edge of his mattress, looking tense. On his night table sat a fully loaded Glock 17. He glanced back and forth between the gun and me. "I love you, Jesse," he told me. "But if you try anything, I will fucking end you."

Every morning at 6:00 Sam woke me up, fed me breakfast (or at least tried to), and then trekked with me downtown to the Broward Addiction Recovery Center (BARC), a beat-down, county-run facility in the heart of Fort Lauderdale's most notorious ghetto. The detox unit was funded by the county and accepted patients on a sliding-scale basis, so beds there were scarce. It was nothing like the nice rehab centers I had been to in the past, but at this point I was broke, un-insured, and addicted. I didn't have many options. Sam and I went down to BARC every day to try to get me a bed, but after a week I was still on the waiting list.

Sam couldn't take any more time off work and needed to hand me off to someone else. My parents wanted nothing to do with me, so I ended up at my grandparents' house. Audrey and Seymour are my maternal grandparents. As a child, I loved going to their house and grilling with Papa Seymour and playing with racecars that he'd picked out just for me. But this wasn't like those childhood visits. I barely spoke to them that night. I just sweated it out in their guest room and then went back to BARC the next morning. This time I lucked out. Some patient had moved on to the next level of treatment, and a bed was finally available for me.

BARC turned out to be straight out of *One Flew over the Cuckoo's Nest*. Fifteen beds were crammed into four dingy, windowless rooms. The common area held a couple of tables where addicts in various stages of withdrawal sat around in hospital scrubs reading newspapers and smoking cigarettes nonstop.

That night I immediately slumped into bed, a shaky, sweaty mess, and mercifully fell asleep. At daybreak a firm hand shook my bed. I rubbed my eyes and put on my glasses, and only then did the full measure of my circumstances come into focus. The concrete walls of the room were painted a ghostly white. My bed was nothing more than a cot with rusted metal legs holding up a sagging layer of wire mesh. The mattress was encased in rubber and covered with a worn, paper-thin sheet. All of the beds around me were filled. Next to me was a thirtysomething derelict who smelled like shit and was mumbling incoherently. His whole body was trembling. I looked up at the tall, pale nurse who was towering over me. "Get up," she commanded. "It's time for your medication."

At BARC I noticed that a small, tender bump in my forearm had moved deep into the muscle, causing my forearm to swell up to twice its normal size. This wasn't my first abscess; junkies get them all the time from dirty needles. I was funded for five days at BARC, after which I received a twenty-eight-day voucher for intensive residential treatment (IRT) in Fort Lauderdale. It was a lot nicer there, and the intake staff took one look at my arm and sent me to the emergency room to have the abscess drained.

At the hospital the doctor opened and drained a golf-ball-size infection, cleaning it out with a long, thin string that looked like a shoelace. The pain was agonizing, but the look on the doctor's face as he attended to me was somehow worse. He looked at me with something worse than disdain. It was indifference. As he worked he didn't say a word, but his expression and mannerisms clearly told me, *You're nothing more than a fucking junkie who's just going to go out and get high again.* More than anything, I wished I disagreed with him.

I passed the time in treatment playing guitar, smoking cigarettes, and trading schemes with other patients. Every afternoon we had group therapy, which was run by Erin, an intense, take-no-crap therapist I had first met during my outpatient therapy at Challenges. Though I'd detoxed away my physical addiction, my urge to use hadn't gone away. A lot of my fellow patients felt the same way. I heard about all sorts of different tools people used to smuggle in drugs— shampoo bottles, clothing, stuffed animals, and food items. There was no end to the addicts' creativity. Drug deals went down regularly even though the grounds had a zero-tolerance policy. The rules didn't matter. Addicts are some of the most resourceful people in the world.

After IRT, I received a voucher for Prospect, a half-way house in the same shady section of Fort Lauderdale as BARC. All residents there were required to find a job and attend outpatient rehab, but I only went to rehab maybe three times. I had more important things on my mind, like finding the best place to score. The unease that had settled back over me when I stopped using was too much to bear. I needed an outlet, and the only one I knew of was drugs.

There was nothing I wouldn't do to score. I was desperate and often victimized my fellow junkies just to get high. I'd first met Dimitri at BARC. He had been using for years, had contracted HIV and hepatitis C from sharing needles, and had recently been diagnosed with cancer. Dimitri was stick-thin with thin wisps of long, scraggly hair partially obscuring his deep-set eyes. His pale skin hung from his face like melted candle wax. Because of his illness, Dimitri had prescriptions for every drug imaginable, and I offered to pay him to get his prescriptions filled. But when we got to the pharmacy, I took his pills and left him zero cash. I didn't have any. As soon as Dimitri's pills ran out, I took off for Miami looking to score. When I got back to Prospect only hours later, I was locked out and found my belongings stuffed in a garbage bag outside the front door.

Needing a place to stay, I showed up at a halfway house called Florida House, holding my garbage bag of belongings and wearing my Oscar-worthy game face. Florida House was run by two guys in recovery who agreed to take me in right away. They were good people who insisted that residents get a job. Before long I landed a sweet gig at Mark's restaurant in Mizner Park. It was never hard to get a job once I said that I had cooked at Smith's. Other chefs respected my former boss and always took me at my word. Mark Milettello was an award-winning chef who'd played a part in creating the New World "Flor-ribbean" cuisine that came out of South Florida in the early '90s. I worked the grill station during lunch, a real wood-burning grill that was one of the hardest to work. It took serious skill to control the temperature on that thing, but I loved feeding the fire.

Once I got paid, I was supposed to turn over part of my check as rent to the guys who ran Florida House, but before even going into work on payday I packed up my stuff. I grabbed my check and called Brad, begging him to let me stay. As soon as he agreed I bolted from Mark's, screwing over my job and the halfway house in the same moment.

I loved staying at Brad's. At night I earned my keep by cooking for him, making the shepherd's pie I had created with Cate years before and the meatloaf I perfected in rehab.

While I was staying there, I got a job at a place called Rino's as the lunch chef. Rino was an Italian-born chef making his way in sunny Florida, and I learned a lot from him about working with pasta and fresh fish. He also taught me more of the rustic Italian cooking techniques I had first admired in Florence, like always starting the garlic in cold olive oil. I played around using the skills I'd picked up at the Asian fusion restaurant with classic Italian ingredients, using hot olive oil instead of sesame to cook a thinly sliced piece of fish.

I had it pretty good at Brad's house, but eventually my appetite for more got the best of me. My drug habit was out of control, and my salary from Rino's alone couldn't sustain it. I started stealing from Brad, and he had no choice but to throw me out. But as angry as he was, he could never throw me to the wolves. "You've got to get the fuck out of here," Brad told me. "I'm dropping you at Victor's."

Victor took me in right away. He and I had grown up together but traveled in completely different circles. By then he had developed a reputation as one of Broward County's top coke dealers. Mostly he dealt at bars and strip clubs, but his source was Carson, a big-time dealer with a well-deserved reputation for violence. Nobody fucked with Carson. When Victor introduced us, he described Carson as his wholesaler.

Cocaine wasn't my thing. All it did was distract me from what I really wanted, which was heroin. One day I had just shot some heroin at Victor's and was feeling good when another friend of ours came by. I saw him putting some coke in a spoon—just like I'd done with the heroin—and asked what he was doing. "It's amazing," he told me simply. "Here, I'll give you a touch." Placing a quarter of a gram in my spoon, he instructed me to let it dissolve instead of cooking it. After I went through the process and shot the coke directly into my arm, I felt a crazy rush that came up through my throat. I could taste it. It was so intense that it almost made me puke. I heard a ringing in my ears and felt chills on the back of my neck, but after two minutes it was gone and I wanted more.

One day soon after that Victor went out and I searched his room until I found a quarter-ounce of coke under his mattress. Over the next few hours I shot all of it, and by the time Victor came home I was chewing my face off. "What the fuck did you do?" he asked me. Before long I learned to mix heroin and coke together, and I got the rush of cocaine and the bliss of heroin all at once, a swarm of warmth and happiness that sucked me in completely.

This was an expensive habit. Our friend Luisa was waitressing at a cheesy wine bar in Coral Springs that I'll call The Grove. I told her that I needed a night job, and she introduced me to the owner, Rodger, who was an ex-cop. His chef had just quit, and he hired me right away. Every morning I left Victor's house and walked across the golf course to work the lunch shift at Rino's, then I walked a couple of blocks to The Grove to start prepping for dinner.

When I got to The Grove, it was a wine bar that served food, but not really a restaurant. The menu consisted of frozen deep-fried appetizers like chicken wings that came straight out of a bag, cheesy chicken tostadas, and potato skins. I was skinny and sick and craving drugs in a bad way, but it was just me in the kitchen, and I managed to be in the moment with the food. Right away I saw how I could improve the menu and the quality of the food we served at The

Grove. I started bringing in fresh chicken wings and making my own clarified butter for the hot sauce instead of using a premixed sauce. The celery and carrots we used sat roughly cut in ten-gallon containers filled with water. After a couple of days they were soggy and gross, so I nixed this and started cutting the vegetables to order so they were always fresh and crispy. When someone rented out the back room for a private party, I took the tostadas and cut them into perfect one-inch batons, fried them, and stood them up on a nice plate with some homemade dipping sauces so they became a proper hors d'oeuvre.

The frozen spinach and artichoke dip that The Grove used came in a container that looked like a mini-Pringles can; when I ripped open the top, it emitted a sulfuric stench, like roasted broccoli that had been sitting out all night. I went to the store and bought some cream and reduced it down until it got nice and thick. Then I added fresh Parmesan cheese. I took whole artichokes and peeled them (much more effectively than I had as a young teen), fried them, and then chopped them up and threw them into the pot along with whole bunches of fresh spinach. I set the mixture to drain overnight, and by the next day it was a thick, delicious dip. Not only did the dip taste better, but making it fresh was also a lot cheaper than buying everything premade. Before long the regulars at The Grove recognized my contributions. "If this place stays open any longer, it will be because of you," they told me.

Despite being completely drowned in drugs, I savored my time in the kitchen, even if I was just frying chicken wings. This was the only time when I wasn't thinking about hustling to score drugs. I temporarily forgot about being dope-sick, my family, and my fucked-up circumstances. For the moment at least, it was just me and the chicken wings.

Some nights Rino came to The Grove for drinks, and I watched him and Rodger out of the corner of my eye, talking about me. I had spent years pulling the wool over everyone's eyes, but I couldn't bullshit Rodger. He knew I had a drug problem and tried to help me by only giving me a little bit of money at a time. It didn't matter. I would have done anything to get drugs. The Grove had a room out back that connected to the restaurant. Inside were shelves stacked with liquor and a couple of refrigerators and freezers that held lobster tails and filet mignon. I stole a key to the back room and made a copy. After work I grabbed as much as I could carry, then met up with dealers and exchanged the food for drugs.

I didn't have a car, so I just walked or took the city bus everywhere, but I was getting sick of this. One of the waiters at Rino's had a 1982 Volvo that he was looking to unload. It had logged over 100,000 miles and was pretty beat-up. "A thousand bucks," he told me.

"I'll give you two hundred dollars now and then two hundred a week for the next four weeks," I replied. I gave him the $200, and he handed me the keys. A week later I quit Rino's and left with the car, never paying the waiter the $800 I still owed him. Now I had wheels and my days free, which I spent either trying to get loaded, being dope-sick, or coming down off a cocaine and heroin frenzy.

This arrangement suited me fine until Victor got arrested for possession of cocaine. Luckily I wasn't around when the arrest went down, but I continued to stay at his house long after he was gone. One day Carson swung by. "Where's Victor?" he wanted to know.

"He got picked up," I told him.

"Bitch better not talk," he replied coldly.

In less than a week there was an eviction notice posted on Victor's door. I started sneaking in through the windows, but one night I came home from working at The Grove and found that the place had been boarded up. The furniture had all been dumped out in the parking lot. I started sleeping in my car behind The Grove, but like I'd done with every other place I'd lived, I didn't take care of it. The oil light had been on for weeks, and the wipers didn't work, but I wasn't going to fix anything; I barely had money for gas. Every penny I earned went straight to drugs.

When Brad heard about Victor's arrest, he came by The Grove one night to check on me. He had forgiven me, probably in part because of his own growing heroin addiction. We quickly patched things up and made plans to score.

Not long after, I was doing about fifty on the Sawgrass Expressway one night when my car died. I put it in neutral and tried turning the engine over a couple of times. Nothing. Cars were lining up behind me, honking their horns, but I couldn't do a thing. I tried turning the engine one more time before it burst and caught on fire. Melted insulation immediately started pouring through the AC vents as I pulled over onto the shoulder. I got out and just started running. When I looked back and saw flames underneath the car, I suddenly remembered that I had left my spoon and needle in the center console. I ran back and opened the car door, dodging flames as I tried to rescue my drug paraphernalia. After grabbing my stuff, I started running again as the car burned. In the distance I heard sirens. I walked the rest of the way to Brad's house and asked him to drive me back to the scene later that night. The car was still there, but it was now nothing more than a pile of smoldering metal.

Claire, a bartender at The Grove, was a recovering junkie. We hit it off, and she took me in, treating me like a son. Whenever I needed to get straight, I showed up at Claire's house, and she fed me, bathed me, and made sure I had clean clothes to wear. She probably would have let me stay there, but her husband hated me. He was about forty years old, with a prosthetic leg, and liked to hit me with his crutch.

Through Claire I met Don, a seventy-year-old former firefighter from Chicago who was a major crackhead. He carried his crack pipe and accessories in a black leather tote bag. I could tell that Don had been smoking for years. He was always coughing, and his eyes were filmy and rimmed with red. Like me, he was always edgy and restless.

Don had managed to wrangle a steady supply of scripts from his doctor and hooked me up with OCs, but I also needed a place to crash. Don owned a house in Deerfield Beach and also had a 5,000-square-foot warehouse in Pompano. Inside was an immaculate, well-maintained saltwater fish tank, but otherwise the place looked like an abandoned shooting gallery. It was filled with an incongruous collection of random tools, discarded tables, empty propane tanks, and file boxes stacked high with paper. There was no heat, air conditioning, or running water, just an outdoor shower connected to an empty propane tank. Don agreed to let me rent a room for a couple of hundred bucks a month.

The warehouse sat on the edge of Dixie Highway and Atlantic Boulevard. After work I wandered around the neighborhood, strung out of my mind. Bored and armed kids congregated on the stoops of abandoned buildings. Others gathered in empty parking lots. Mothers pushed their crying babies in strollers late into the night. The locals fucked with me all the time, but I just scrounged the ground for discarded cigarette butts, anything to keep the buzz going and drown out the reality of my life.

My car was gone, and to get to The Grove from the warehouse I had to take two buses. My shift started at six, so I had to drag my ass out of bed by four to get there in time. One day I woke up really dope-sick. I was burning up and sweating profusely, but I was also incredibly cold. The damp air inside Don's filthy warehouse felt like a hundred razor blades raking my skin. I stayed in bed and never showed up to work at The Grove.

Brad came to see me soon after and told me he had moved into a new apartment. He seemed to feel bad about what had gone down and was willing to let me stay with him. His timing was perfect. I hadn't paid Don in weeks, and he changed the locks the very next day. A few days after arriving at Brad's, he drove me back to the warehouse to get my stuff. I knocked on the door. No one answered, but I could hear feet shuffling inside. I knew Don was in there. "Don, it's Jesse," I called. "Open the door. I just want to get my shit and leave." Minutes passed before Don finally opened the door. He stood there, naked except for a thin gold chain dangling from his neck, mumbling incoherently. He was tweaking out of his mind.

I walked past Don and went inside. There was a pit bull barking in the far corner of the warehouse and the floor was covered in dog shit. A young woman was lying on a small wooden coffee table, passed out. She was maybe eighteen or nineteen years old, and was completely naked. I quickly grabbed my stuff and split.

This whole time I had been on probation as part of my sentence for narcotics trafficking. It had been months since I checked in with my probation officer. In the eyes of the law, I was a fugitive.

Brad worked during the day fixing roofs, and since I was now out of a job, I went along with him. My first order of business when we arrived at a job was always to check the medicine cabinet for any drugs I could score. Brad and I got high every day together. One day we were out on a job when Victor's wholesaler, Carson, called me and asked if I wanted to run for him. It sounded like a good deal. I'd get drugs and money. I said yes right away.

Carson gave me a car and a phone and I started as his runner. I dropped off drugs and collected money from dozens of buyers every day, and in exchange Carson gave me drugs. Everything was copacetic until one Sunday. Brad and I were still coming down from the night before when there was a knock on the door. It was Carson. By his feet was a small gray safe. "There's heat on me," he told me. "You need to look after this." I looked at the safe, knowing it was full of money and drugs. What else could have been in there? "Don't open it," Carson warned.

The minute Carson walked out the door I called a locksmith, who got the safe open. I threw him an extra $50 from the safe so he would look the other way. Brad and I took the rest of the safe's contents and went on a major binge, staying home for days just shooting cocaine. We started hallucinating snipers in front of the apartment and helicopters circling overhead. All we did was get high. We drove to Miami to score with Carson's money and pulled into the gas station to fix in the bathroom on the way there. When I got back to Brad's car, I carefully placed my needle and spoon in one of his tool kits.

There was a knock on the car window what seemed like moments later. I was asleep in the front seat with no idea how long I'd been out. I looked up and saw cops. They had just found Brad in the bathroom with a needle in his pocket and arrested him on the spot. Brad begged the cops to leave me alone. He knew I was on probation and somehow convinced them that I wasn't involved, saving my ass in the process. I left the gas station with his car and bailed him out the next day. We went right back to our daily binges.

I was no longer running for Carson, and we had already gone through all of the drugs and money in the safe, so I needed to get a job. I landed a gig at Max's Grille in Mizner Park. Max's was a South Florida institution. It had been around forever, and every South Florida chef who was anybody had started out working for its founder, Dennis Max. It was always crazy busy there; a thousand covers a day was the norm. I worked the salad station and the vegetable station and was basically the bitch. I made plate after plate of sautéed spinach and bowl after bowl of the Caesar salad that came with the prix fixe dinner special. Once 5:00 P.M. hit, that printer would not stop. Ticket after ticket came spewing out, and we'd get slammed. I had a hot pan on the stove next to a huge pot of water and a ladle. Every time an order came in, I put a huge bunch of spinach into the pan with a little bit of butter. Then I added a ladleful of the hot water so it would sauté down quickly. There was a reach-in refrigerator on the wall holding the romaine lettuce, so when an order for the Caesar salad came in, I could reach into a door right next to my head and grab what I needed. I did this roughly five hundred times a night.

Every night before leaving work I called Brad and asked, "Should I stop off and get some dope?" I don't know why I even asked. The answer was always the same. An hour later I'd show up at Brad's place with dope and leftover food. Meatloaf and mashed potatoes were still his favorites.

Sometimes when Brad and I bought drugs together, we couldn't even make it home without getting high. The Holiday Inn right off Commercial Boulevard and I-95 was our favorite place to stop. One night we made our way to the bathroom with some heroin that was dark brown and the consistency of bird shit. Brad did two bags, but I stuck with one. "Fuck," Brad said from his stall. "I should've done one." Suddenly, I heard a thump. I dropped to my knees and peeked under the stall. Brad was just lying there with a needle sticking out of his track-marked forearm and his pants down around his ankles. The stall door was locked. I was high, but somehow I managed to crawl underneath the stall to try to wake him up. No response. I slapped him across the face. Still nothing. I ran from the bathroom to the front desk.

"My friend is passed out in the bathroom," I told the concierge. He called 911, and five minutes later security entered the bathroom. They injected Brad with something, and he immediately started vomiting before they took him off to the hospital.

Of course, by then Carson realized that I had robbed him blind. I had been ducking his phone calls, but I knew that wouldn't buy me much time. That night, when Brad was in the hospital, Carson came knocking. I opened the door not knowing what to expect, and took three hard punches to the face that knocked me over the couch before I came crashing into an end table. He grabbed everything he could get his hands on—the computer, TV, stereo. When I picked Brad up from the hospital, I told him what happened. That was it for Brad. He wanted out. He moved back in with his mother, leaving me alone in the apartment.

All of my money from Max's was going to buying drugs, and without Brad there to pay the bills, there was soon no hot water or electricity. An eviction notice wasn't far behind. For a month I became a squatter, sneaking in and out of the run-down apartment. When I was there, I holed up inside and shot up crushed pain pills.

Every few days I snuck out and took the bus to the new bar where Claire was now working. She fed me, gave me drinks, and tried to make sure I was okay. There I met a waitress named Tonya who was looking for a roommate and said I could bunk with her. My first night there Tonya said, "Jess, I'm going out for some coke. You cool with that?"

"I hope you don't mind," I said, "but I like to shoot it."

Tonya and I fell into a routine of doing coke together: she'd snort it and I'd shoot it, and then we'd spend the rest of the day hanging out and listening to music. Before long I quit working at Max's. I was always dope-sick and couldn't make it in. But they still owed me my final check. I told Tonya that I'd make good on the rent as soon as I got paid, but she never saw a dime. It didn't take long for her to kick me out.

I took that final check from Max's, scored some dope, and used what was left to rent an efficiency on Deerfield Beach. This was the place of last resort, just a small step above a cardboard box. My room was tiny, the walls were paper-thin, and the bed was covered in stained nylon sheets. Cops were always stopping by and arresting people for assault, domestic violence, or murder, and even for running a meth lab out of one of the rooms. I couldn't believe the shit that was going on around me.

I spent my first two days getting high and the next five coming down. Detoxing was hell, but I had been through it before. I was out of money, alone, and feeling pretty desperate when I called Sam. He rode over on his motorcycle and couldn't believe how I was living. He took me to the store to buy groceries, and then we sat outside for hours, drinking beers by the empty swimming pool. A week later I couldn't pay my rent and got kicked out.

It had been a year since I'd seen or heard from my parents. In that time I had bounced around from place to place, but I had never actually slept on the street. But this time I really had no place to go. I was officially homeless.

CHAPTER SEVEN

Entremets

Entremets: A small dish served in between the main courses of a meal.

I stood outside of a 7-Eleven on Deerfield Beach, broke and alone, with nowhere to go and without a friend in the world. I can't say I didn't deserve it. My need for drugs had so consumed me that by then I had lied, cheated, and stolen from every friend and family member I had. Every time someone had tried to help me, I'd bitten the hand that fed me.

That night I walked down the highway for hours until I found South Beach Park, which had a running trail, high scrubs, ficus trees, and tons of mulch. I lay down on the cleanest patch of grass I could find and stared up at the stars until I fell asleep. The next morning I awoke to the nudge of a rake in my hip. It was the park ranger, wanting me out. I was covered in mosquito bites, dirty, and hungry. I needed to find work.

I walked to a restaurant called Pranzo's in Mizner Park, but before going in I went into a Burger King. In the bathroom I splashed my face, combed back my hair with my wet fingers, and did my best to scrub the dirt out from underneath my nails. The chef at Pranzo's was a nice guy. As I was talking to him I had to hold myself back from scratching the mosquito bites that lined my torso and back from sleeping in the grass. I told the chef that I needed a job and had fallen on hard times. He was impressed with my previous work experience and found a spot for me. "Be here at three today," he said.

It felt good to stand behind the line again that night. The restaurant's biggest sellers were Spaghetti Carbonara and Rigatoni with Caponata. My imagination immediately perked up. The caponata was too sweet. I wanted to add more vinegar and maybe some pine nuts, but I was too distracted to even try talking to the chef. I had to find a place to sleep that night.

After work I walked around looking for options. At another 7-Eleven on Dixie Highway, I approached a couple of guys who looked to be in their fifties. One of them was hunched over with a filter dangling from his lips as he scoured the ground for discarded cigarette butts. The other guy was tall and thin and smelled, quite literally, like shit. He didn't say a word; he just growled. "Where do you fuckers sleep?" I asked.

"I'm Ralph," said the one who talked. "His name is Bobbie 'the Flame' Tucker." I introduced myself. "Why don't you sit down, kid?" Ralph asked. As we talked he handed me a beer. After a while we got up and walked to a meter room in the parking garage of a nearby shopping plaza. It was home to an industrial-sized Dumpster. Bobbie pulled out four huge Burger King French fry boxes and laid them out neatly on the floor. This was his bedding.

The next day I was awake at 6:00 A.M. and didn't have to

be at work until 3:00. The waiting game was a killer. I walked into a deli across the street to apply for a job. The manager handed me the application, but I only got as far as the section that read, "Address." I couldn't fill it in. The manager and I started talking, and it turned out that he and the entire staff were in recovery, living in a halfway house just up the street.

"One of my guys just gave notice," he told me. "You can start in two weeks."

Over the next two weeks I hung out with Ralph and Bobbie the Flame and some of their homeless buddies. One night we were sitting on the embankment next to the train tracks. It must have been ten or eleven, not the middle of the night but late enough so there weren't a lot of people out. Bobbie was on the other side of the tracks, and as the lights started blinking to indicate a train was coming he started walking toward us, limping as usual. Just as the guardrail was closing, a car sped underneath it and drove into Bobbie. It ran right over him and just kept going. I was horrified, but one thing I learned being on the street was not to get involved in shit. In shock, I just took off before the cops showed up.

On the day I was set to start work at the deli I walked in around 7:00 A.M. There were two guys behind the counter, one who looked barely seventeen, and another who was short and burly with a few teeth missing. "You must be the new guy," he said with a thick New York accent. "I'm Joey."

I walked behind the counter and surveyed the scene. The place needed a fucking cleanup. I spent the next four hours scrubbing the floors, organizing the fridges, and cleaning the slicer. It was a good first day at work. On my way out to go to Pranzo's, I saw two of the guys from the deli smoking cigarettes. One of them started to curl over and close his eyes a little bit. I knew that look too well. "What the fuck are you on, bro?" I asked him. "I want some."

"Nothing, man, nothing," he insisted.

"Bullshit," I spat out. "What is it? Percs? Oxy?"

"No," he said finally. "Methadone wafers."

"Shit," I said. This was music to my ears. "Hook me up." He gave me the number of a girl who had a script and would sell them for $20 a wafer. I called her that Friday as soon as I got my first paycheck from the deli. I had two jobs and no place to stay, but I literally cared more about having drugs than even a roof over my head. Weeks passed. I worked at the deli during the day and at Pranzo's at night. In between I went to see movies or found a way to score. I ate at work, so I never had to worry about food, but at night I slept outside, swathed in a blanket of newspaper. Before going to sleep on a bench or in the bushes, I'd take a methadone wafer and then chain-smoke all night. I often woke up with cigarette burns covering my chest.

After two months I was fully addicted again and stopped showing up at Pranzo's. My check from the deli didn't amount to much, and I was hurting, so I took to panhandling outside of fast-food restaurants, where there was always someone coming in or going out. One day I was outside a Burger King, not having much luck, when a Latino guy started talking to me. I told him a sob story about losing my job and getting thrown out by my parents.

"Walk with me," he said. As we walked he told me that his name was Julio. He had come to the United States illegally from Nicaragua after the civil unrest and had gotten by sleeping near construction sites until he made his way in the States. "You can stay at my place," he said. "How's a hundred dollars a month?" It all sounded a little too easy, but I wasn't in a position to argue. Julio's apartment was small, just a couple of rooms, but it did have a balcony with a sweet ocean view.

"I don't have a mattress for you," Julio said, "but you can sleep in the bed with me and my roommate Juan." Right away, I knew exactly what he was looking for. Sure enough, after the three of us climbed into the apartment's only bed that night, I woke up to find Julio practically on top of me. I jumped up and turned on the light.

"Dude, that's not fucking happening," I told him.

"I just want your ass," he replied calmly.

After that, I set down some pretty firm boundaries. "I will sleep on the floor in the living room," I told him, "and I'll give you a hundred bucks to do so." Julio never came on to me again. I acquired an air mattress to sleep on in the living room. I did learn a few tricks from him and Juan, though, particularly where men would go to solicit sex. Juan introduced me to his friend who was basically a pimp. He set me up with a location and told me that most of the older men were looking for young kids like me.

After I'd been standing in my spot for just a few minutes, a dark car approached. I walked over and found a man inside who was at least fifty years old, wearing a business suit and a platinum wedding ring. "Fifty," I told him. He nodded in response. I got in and closed the door. "Put the money in the center console," I said. He already had the cash in his hands. Then I said, "Pull your dick out and pull your pants down around your ankles." I moved over as if I was about to give him a blow job, waiting for him to close his eyes. Then I grabbed the money and ran. Looking back, I could see that he was pissed, but he couldn't come after me with his pants down.

I met Gibson at the deli. He had just finished serving five years in prison for armed robbery and was a stone-cold crack addict. I was shooting a little cocaine and taking the methadone wafers when I could get them. During breaks I fixed in the deli's bathroom. One night Gibson approached me and said, "I want to get high."

The girl I had been buying the methadone wafers from had been telling me that crack was the way to go. One night she drove Gibson and me to Oakland Park. "Just wait here," she said after parking the car. A few minutes later she came back carrying a clear bag filled with something resembling soap shavings. Getting in the car, she reached under the driver's seat and produced a pipe, a hollowed-out tire gauge, a lighter, and a copper Brillo pad, which crackheads use for filters. She lit up, took a hit, and passed the pipe to Gibson. As he took a hit I looked into his eyes. He was done. With one hit, he morphed from a nice, easygoing guy into an absolute destroyer.

My turn. I placed a large piece of crack in the top, holding the pipe carefully so it didn't fall out, then lit the pipe and slowly inhaled. The rock crackled slightly, making a sound that reminded me of cold milk hitting a bowl of Rice Krispies. In my lungs the smoke was slightly unpleasant, and it smelled like burned rubber or an electrical fire. When I blew out the smoke, the sensation hit, an intense, euphoric rush like sticking my head out the window of a fighter jet. It was as good as shooting coke, but cheaper and easier to get. And it took less than a minute for the magic to kick in.

The only downside was that the high only lasted a few minutes. I spent the next few months chasing the feeling of that first hit. Soon I couldn't hold down the job at the deli and got fired. Out of money, I robbed Julio and all of his friends and got kicked out of the apartment. Gibson and I were on a run, stealing from motel rooms and even from drug dealers. Another trap door had opened, and I continued to fall.

CHAPTER EIGHT

Pressure Cooker

Pressure cooker: A sealed vessel used to cook food in hot water or other cooking liquid. Because pressure cookers do not allow air or liquids to escape below a preset level of pressure, the steam inside from the boiling liquid permeates the food and heats it more quickly than other methods do.

Save for the low, incessant humming of exhaust fans that poured out a noxious concoction of gas and bacon grease from some hole-in-the-wall diner, an odd silence hung in the air as thick and heavy as any South Florida summer evening. Gibson and I had made our way back "home," which in this case was a motel that sat directly across from the Fort Lauderdale Amtrak station. The motel's green-brick facade was stained and chipped, with boards covering many of its windows and graffiti adorning the walls. The motel marquee, rusted and weather-beaten beyond recognition, lay awkwardly on the sidewalk. Out back sat a dirty, leaf-filled rectangular swimming pool that hadn't been filled in years. Weeds choked the motel parking lot's cracked, scarred pavement, home to a couple of cars, lookouts, scantily clad prostitutes, forsaken drug paraphernalia, and a small militia of rats, mice, and palmetto bugs.

The motel was a melting pot of dealers, prostitutes, and addicts, mixed in with a few destitute immigrant families and one elderly couple who had moved in after losing their home. Some mornings I woke up to find a nude chick passed out in the front yard or a dealer bolting out the door with a gun barely concealed under his jacket. The nights were filled with the sounds of screeching brakes and blaring sirens. Coming down from my latest fix, I just lay there unable to sleep, listening to the regular assortment of shouts and arguments from neighboring rooms. Or I peeled open the curtains and stared out through the grimy glass of our partially shattered window and watched people rush to and from the station, wondering who they were and where they were going.

This was shit-hole central. It was pure chaos, and Gibson and I fit right in. After taking a hit, we would tear the fucking place apart, dumping out trash cans, searching behind the toilet, and ripping open sofa cushions looking for crack. I spent hours crawling around that dirty rug, tweaking out of my mind, searching for an imaginary piece of crack I was sure I'd dropped. There was never any crack, but one time I found pieces of soap, stuck them in a pipe, and promptly puked all over the floor. Crack looks like soap shavings, except it's sharp. I'd run through a bar of Dove in the blink of an eye.

By then I was shooting dope four or five times a day. I had to keep it up so I didn't get sick. My day-to-day struggle was to get straight, but of course once I straightened out and was feeling better I was back on the hunt for more.

The motel was awful, but we had paid in advance to stay there for two months. This felt like a luxury after sleeping on the street for over a year. The motel gave me the two things every addict needs: comfort and time. Every day we had to pull off some sort of heist so we'd have money to get high. Sometimes we hit up a laundromat and smashed the change dispensers. Other times we walked through a nice neighborhood, found an open car door, and took whatever was inside. I was always surprised by what people left in their cars—money, jewelry, credit cards, computers, cell phones—and we grabbed all of it.

But our biggest hustle was following dealers. We watched one guy's house for weeks, learning his habits—when he normally picked up his deliveries and when he got his cash. We knew exactly when he'd be getting home with his cash from the bank and showed up to his house to find his pickup truck in the driveway still running. Without wasting a moment, Gibson and I jumped into his truck and drove away, not stopping until we were miles from the house. Finally, we searched the car and found a bank envelope under the seat containing $10,000 in cash.

We kept the car for a few days, driving around to different ghettos and approaching dealers on bikes. "Show us what you got," I said to the dealers. When they stuck their hand in the car window holding a bag of crack to show it to us, I'd slap their hand and drive off as the bag of crack fell into my lap. Gibson wanted to keep the truck, but there was a warrant out for my arrest and I saw no reason to be driving around in a stolen truck. I convinced him to abandon it one night in an empty parking lot.

The crack we stole from those small-time dealers in Fort Lauderdale was always cut or bulked or buffered with laxatives, Benadryl, sugar, starch, talc, brick dust, or even fucking Ajax. Drugs are almost always cut with something else. Some dealers want to make it go further; others just want to charge more. This leads to all different breeds of crack, coke, and heroin. Our buddy Dan who was living in Orlando told us they had shit there that was higher up on the food chain. "This is pure shit that hasn't been stepped on a million times," he told us.

We had ten grand burning a hole in our pockets, and this sounded worthy of a trip. After a long 220-mile, drug-fueled cab ride from Fort Lauderdale to Orlando, we checked into a motel and spent the night smoking and shooting. By morning we were tweaking out of our minds. With crack, the high doesn't last long. Right away you just start freaking out. Your pupils dilate, your speech slows, and you start hearing and seeing things that no one else does. It's a psychotic state that you're completely aware of but can't do anything to change.

Out of crack, we headed for the Orange Blossom Trail, a major road that's famous for its notorious drug crime. Almost immediately, we saw some young drug dealers. "We're looking for some hard," Gibson told them.

"You a narc?" asked one kid who seemed to be the leader. I didn't blame the kid for being suspicious of two white guys in this neighborhood.

"No," Gibson said, but the kids didn't believe him. "Get the fuck out of here," the leader told us. "I mean it." Before we could move he pulled out a gun and started shooting into the air, letting us know that he was serious. Gibson and I took off, running as fast as we could as the sounds of gunfire still echoed in the distance. It was only ten or eleven in the morning, but the sun was already blazing relentlessly in a cloudless blue sky. There wasn't even the slightest hint of wind, nothing to cool the scorching heat. My soiled, soaked clothes were caked to my body; my hair was a matted fucking mess. As I ran sweat bubbled from my forehead, stinging my ears and smearing my glasses, which dangled perilously close to the tip of my nose.

Finally, Gibson and I stopped, panting and completely out of breath. We couldn't hear the gunfire anymore. When we looked behind us, there was no one in sight. Quickly, we made our way off the tracks and down a hill of gravel, weeds, and packed, dry dirt. Right away we stumbled across a guy sitting alone, smoking Black & Milds, with his feet propped up on a weather-beaten milk crate. He was lean and lanky, with fetid dreadlocks framing his narrow face. The vague silhouette of a gun was visible beneath his many layers of clothes.

"We're looking for some hard," Gibson said once again. Without uttering a syllable or even looking up, Mr. Dreads got up and started walking. We followed him a few hundred feet through some bushes to a clearing that led to a littered parking lot, and beyond, a wretched bilevel motel with peeling paint on the green-and-blue doors. All over the parking lot were lookouts—ten-year-old kids on bikes who spent their days popping wheelies and warning dealers when the police showed up. "One time, two time," they called out, depending on how many cops they spotted. The kids saw us, nodded their approval, and backed away.

Mr. Dreads guided us through the motel parking lot, navigating a path carved of cars, lookouts, pint-sized prostitutes, and addicts, until we arrived at room number 4. He knocked on the door three times and left without saying a word. The door opened, and we walked in. Quickly the door closed behind us. The room was dark save for a lone lightbulb hanging from a broken ceiling fixture. The curtains were drawn, but I could still make out the staccato blink of the motel's red-and-white neon marquee. On a table in the center of the room were a couple dozen clear plastic bags, a gun, and two small stacks of cash.

"You a fucking narc?" The dealer was wiry and anxious. A thick, shiny gold chain dangled from his neck, and a stack of small gold bracelets circled his wrists. He grabbed the gun from the table and pressed the cold steel barrel to my temple.

"I just want crack," I said. Slowly, and I mean really fucking slowly, I pulled $200 out of my pocket and placed it down on the bed. Crack was the only fucking thing on my mind. But the dealer didn't know that, and dealers are always suspicious of white boys. I knew he could just shoot me. It would have been easy. That room hadn't been cleaned in years, and it would probably take days before anyone discovered our bodies. After sizing us up for what seemed like forever, the dealer slowly lowered the gun and walked over to the nightstand. Methodically, he pulled open the drawer, reached in, and produced a small, clear bag holding a couple of white, pebble-sized pieces of crack.

Once we had our stash, we needed a room. We couldn't wait long enough to get back to the motel where we'd already checked in. The lobby of this motel was spilling over with brochures for Disney World, Gatorland, Sea World, Sleuths Mystery Dinner Shows, and a dozen other Orlando attractions that we couldn't have cared less about. Sitting behind a thin layer of grimy Plexiglas sat a miserable-looking young woman. "Twenty-nine ninety-five," she said without looking up.

The chairs, curtains, carpets, and sheets in our room were covered in cigarette burns. There were holes in the wall, the bedspread was peppered with dark spots, the drawer handles were all broken, and someone had scribbled profanity all over the room's lone wooden desk. The bathroom reeked of urine and mildew. The sink drain was clogged with cigarette butts, and there was a hypodermic needle on the floor next to the toilet. But we barely noticed any of this as we packed our prize into a thin, smoke-stained glass tube. I inhaled deeply, closing my eyelids as I drew in smoke. Gibson swiped the pipe, took a hit, and then handed it back to me so I could take another drag. Soon we were both wired. Stick-thin Gibson, with his hollow cheekbones and tattooed arms dotted with track marks, started pacing around the room, pausing only to take another puff.

Crack gave me a short-lived euphoria followed immediately by an intense bout of depression. This made it even more addictive than the high, because the only thing that helped me get out of this depression was, of course, more crack. Once I was hooked, I just kept sinking. It didn't take long for the paranoia to kick in, maybe a couple of minutes. We each took a last pull on the pipe before the paranoia settled in, and we were both tweaking, just freaking out. The sirens were wailing. The walls were closing in. Someone would be coming through the door any minute. We needed to get the hell out of that room.

We quickly grabbed our stuff and bolted for the door. Just as we were leaving the motel, we ran straight into a local cop. He was clearly in no mood for bullshit. "What are you doing in this neighborhood?" he asked us in a thick, cartoonishly Southern drawl.

"We're lost," I told him. "We're looking for the bus stop." I don't know how we fooled him. Our eyes were bulging like crazy, and we were jittery, fidgeting like mad, and talking nonstop.

"Don't move," the cop told us. "Wait here." He went to run our names, and we stood there freaking out until he came back empty. If we had been in Fort Lauderdale, we would've been in handcuffs in the back of the squad car. Instead he told us, "You guys have to get out of here now." Then he kindly gave us directions to the city bus, which dropped us off right at our hotel.

By the time we were back in our hotel room, we already wanted more. I called Dan, who'd encouraged us to come to Orlando in the first place. "We've got cash," I told him. "Get us as many bags of dope as you can."

"These are big fucking bags," he cautioned.

"Fuck that," I told him. "Just bring me the mother lode."

Dan pulled up in front of our hotel soon after. Stocky, handsome, and covered in ink, Dan didn't look like an addict, but he'd been a fuck-up for as long as I'd known him.

Gibson and I jumped into Dan's car and drove with him to his apartment. His girlfriend Natasha answered the door wearing a tight tank top over a black bra with a broken strap and blue shorts. She was friendly but awkward. "Hi," she said distractedly while rummaging in her bag for cigarettes. The apartment had old Formica cabinets, cheap plastic flooring, and shag carpeting that looked like it was out of a 1970s porn flick. The dirty white walls were chipping from top to bottom, and cracks in the windows were covered over with pieces of cardboard and Scotch tape. Outside, it was ninety-five and sunny, but inside the shades were drawn and it might as well have been midnight.

Dan grabbed our money and split to meet the dealer, returning an hour later with the dope in hand. Gibson, Natasha, and I sat around a wobbly bridge table with our fingers tapping, legs twitching, and eyes darting in every direction. We were jonesing out of our fucking minds. Dan tossed the bags on the table, and on cue Natasha bit off the end of an unlit cigarette and pulled out the filter.

Heroin isn't like coke or meth. You can't just inject it. First, it has to dissolve in water. In unison the four of us bit open our bags, tasted the heroin, gagged, and then emptied it into a spoon. Then we drew water into the syringes, filled the spoons until the heroin drowned, and lit a match. When I was on the streets and didn't have a spoon or fresh water, I used water from a puddle or a public toilet. Once little bubbles started forming in the cooker, we each took a piece of a cigarette filter and stuck it in the liquid, careful to steady our spoons with one hand while guiding the tips of the needles into the filter with the other. Once our syringes were filled, we turned them upside down so the air bubbles would float to the top, and then we pushed the plungers to remove any lingering bubbles and to get the dope as close to the tips of the needles as possible.

Now it was time to find a good vein. This can be a problem if you've been using for a while. I knew some guys whose arms got so fucked up that they'd shoot right into the jugular. By then I was a vein expert. I made contact, watched my blood snake into the syringe, and pulled the trigger. A surge of hot liquid quickly moved up my arm. My body tingled, and I felt a spike of adrenaline that consumed my brain in a single bite. There's no mistake when the rush hits. It's like a massive orgasm, only better. All my tension melted away, and I spent the next several hours in a warm, cozy state. Every need or desire seemed fulfilled.

Dan, Natasha, and Gibson each did one bag, but I insisted on doing two. I was voracious. But before I could finish shooting the second bag, everything suddenly faded to black.

As my eyes slowly opened—I don't know how much later—faint rays of light from a sputtering bulb came into view. The sound of water dripping from the broken showerhead echoed in my ears. Sights and sounds are always magnified when you come to after falling out. It's like turning on a light switch. I never had any concept of time when I was high. It felt like I'd been out for hours, but it had probably only been a few minutes.

It took a while for my eyes to recognize where I was: lying on a cold bathroom floor, wet, and naked except for my underwear. My left leg was draped over the bathtub. I had no idea how I'd gotten there or why I couldn't move. The left side of my face was swollen and throbbing. Pus was oozing from an abscess on my left forearm. But I was preoccupied with a thick layer of dried blood caked to my right hand. I tried rubbing it off, and a shooting pain shot up my arm.

Eventually I peeled my body off the floor and placed my hand on the wall to steady myself. I stood there looking at myself in the bathroom mirror. My eyes were bloodshot and teary, so dilated they looked like they had no pupils. My gaunt, almost skeletal face had a dull, grayish hue. I didn't recognize that reflection as myself at all.

As I stumbled out of the bathroom I saw Natasha pacing around the room. "What are we gonna do?" she asked Dan. "I think he's fucking dead." Gibson was slumped on the couch, fucked up out of his mind. Surrounding Gibson's bare feet were broken pieces of the coffee table. Slowly I put it all together: I must have taken a header on the coffee table as I'd fallen out, and then Dan and Natasha must have stripped off my clothes and tossed me into the shower, trying to get me to come to.

When Dan and Natasha saw me standing there, Natasha quickly rushed over and gave me a hug. Then she and Dan started wrapping me in a towel. "Guys, I'm good," I told them. As soon as Dan saw that I was indeed okay, he started in with a lecture. "I told you the bags we get in Fort Lauderdale aren't anything like these. You've gotta watch your shit."

I didn't pay much attention, even when Natasha told me that I had stopped breathing and started turning blue. I knew falling out happened all the time; it was a junkie occupational hazard. I was more concerned with the fact that I didn't get any rush this go-round. There was no relief, no warm feeling, nothing. The pain, fear, tension, and anxiety I'd been running from my whole life were right there staring me in the face. "Where's the rest of the dope?" I asked. "I'm ready to go again."

Dan drove Gibson and me back to the hotel, and we spent the next few hours on a dope and crack bender. This time Gibson fell out. He turned blue, and his pulse slowed to a crawl, but I walked him around the room and slapped him across the face until he came to. Then we were ready to go at it again.

By morning we were out of crack again and tweaking out as we chain-smoked cigarettes and paced back and forth, talking a mile a minute. We were also horny as hell, a side effect of the crack. Crack is like sex, but without actually having sex. We started scouring the phone book, looking for hookers, with the singular focus of two crackheads. After a while we got in touch with one chick who told us that she was into some pretty wild shit. "Come over now," I told her.

When she showed up an hour later, she was everything I wanted her to be, with long, silky dark hair, clear porcelain skin, and massive gravity-defying tits. "I'll do anything for two hundred," she told us. We put the money on the nightstand, and she started taking off her clothes. Gibson and I just sat there like fucking zombies. I was half awake, scratching my face, as Gibson started hitting the pipe again. Watching us, she quickly got dressed, grabbed our cash, and made a beeline for the door. "Dude, what the fuck? We just got robbed," Gibson said, but he didn't even bother to move. I got up slowly and stumbled toward the door, but she was already gone.

Getting robbed is a way of life for junkies. We're always either robbing someone else or being robbed by them. I shrugged it off and shifted focus back to getting laid. Rifling through the phonebook, I called about thirty different numbers, but they were all routed to the same location. Half an hour and twenty calls later, I heard a girl in the background say to her friend, "These crackheads keep calling." Eventually we just gave up.

As the first rays of dawn trickled underneath the drawn shades of our hotel room, we finally ran out of crack. We called a taxi and said, "Take us to the worst fucking neighborhood." The cabbie took off without saying a word. A few minutes later we pulled in to a massive forty-lane gas station and truck stop. The cabbie pointed in the direction of a trailer park. "Keep the meter running," Gibson said, handing over fifty bucks. We walked down a narrow path through tons of shady shrubs before approaching a brightly lit trailer with a dented red pickup out front. Outside of the trailer a group of guys sat around drinking beers and smoking cigarettes.

"We're looking for some hard," I told them.

"You a narc?"

"We just want crack," Gibson said impatiently. Finally one guy got up and disappeared into the trailer, then reappeared thirty seconds later holding two small sandwich bags.

We got back in the cab. "We're looking for a hooker," I told the driver, and he handed me a card with a name and number scribbled on the back. As soon as we got back to the hotel we called her up. "What are you into, honey?" Her thick, raspy voice sounded like it had been dipped in syrup. An hour later she knocked on the door. She was probably in her thirties but looked a decade older, with a drawn face earned by years of hard living.

After getting a condom from one of the machines in the lobby, I went back to the room to find Gibson in the bathroom doing a hit. The smoke wafted into the bedroom. We started having sex, but I was so fucked up that I kept losing my erection. "I'm charging double," she said. There was that line again. "Just take the money and get the fuck out," I told her. We were in Orlando for only three days, but we made at least three more trips to the trailer park to score. We managed to blow through the entire ten grand and had no way to get back to Fort Lauderdale. Finally we hustled a ride with Natasha's sister and her husband in their beat-up blue minivan.

After getting back from Orlando, I knew I needed to chill. I hadn't slept in days. "Let's just get some sleep and start over," I told Gibson, but he was like the Energizer Bunny. He just wanted to keep going. "I need to score," he replied and was out the door before I could say anything.

With Gibson gone, I sat down on the bed and closed my eyes. I had been on the street for more than a year. Every morning I woke up not knowing if I would live or die, whether I would eat anything that day or find a safe place to sleep that night. My body was thin and pale, my arms a patchwork of track marks, abscesses, and collapsed veins. Even my ears were permanently deformed from sleeping on concrete and Chattahoochee rock. But my soul was in far worse shape. For years I'd been lying, cheating, and stealing from everyone I had come in contact with. I had no integrity, no genuine relationships, and not an ounce of respect for myself. This existence was wearing me down.

For me, addiction was never really about the substance. It was about the stuff that lay beneath the surface—the tension and anxiety that I'd tried to escape by peeling the wallpaper off my walls as a toddler and later by creating something spectacular in the kitchen. But drugs were the very best escape from myself. Until now. It had once been exciting to chase the next high, but the fun was long gone now. Every time I thought I had hit bottom over the past few years, another trap door opened and I fell further still. But now I knew with absolute certainty that if I kept using I'd wind up either dead or put away for life. There was no further to fall from here.

Sitting there, I had what felt like a moment of clarity. I remembered my dad telling me years earlier, "Drugs or family, Jesse. You can't have both." At the time it had been a no-brainer. I needed drugs to survive, and I didn't give a shit what my dad thought. But the truth was that I missed my family. I missed being loved and cared for, however imperfectly, and most of all I missed caring even the slightest bit about myself. My heart and my conscience, which had been clenched so tightly in the grip of addiction, were slowly starting to return.

I woke up the next morning to the sound of kids playing in the motel's hallway. I could barely move from the bed. I was hot and sweating profusely, as if my skin was on fire, but I also felt incredibly cold. My stomach cramped intermittently with a sharp, stabbing pain that felt like someone was poking it with the tip of a paring knife. Razor blades raked my skin as every muscle in my body twitched uncontrollably. I needed to purge, but I didn't have the energy to even lift my head.

Of course, I knew the one thing that would make me feel better, but for once I didn't want to find someone to rob, scam, or hustle to get money to buy drugs. The hours of insanity suddenly didn't seem worth it for just a few moments of pleasure. I knew that after I scored I'd be right back here in no time, dope-sick and needing to start the whole tortuous process over again. I was on my hands and knees, writhing in pain, and without thinking about it I found myself uttering a plea that sounded like a prayer. I begged whoever was listening to help save me from sinking any further into the quicksand my life had become.

I had toyed around with getting clean a million times before, but I knew this time was it. I was ready to surrender, prepared to choose family over drugs. For years I'd done everything I could to get high, and now I knew I'd do anything to get clean. I picked up the motel room phone and called my parents' house. My mother answered, but when she heard my voice she hung up before I could utter another word. Right away I called back. This time my dad picked up the phone. "Jesse," he said. "I can't help you. Go to Broward General."

I hung up the phone, sobbing uncontrollably. I was twenty-one years old, broke, sick, wanted by the cops, and unwanted by my family. Inside, I was filled with a combination of torment, rage, and mostly pain. To this day I don't know how my parents found the strength to do what they did, but they saved my life.

CHAPTER NINE

Fond

Fond: The roasted bits of meat left at the bottom of a pan when sautéing at a high temperature.

I knew I had hit bottom, but I didn't know how to climb back up yet. My body needed drugs to survive, and my brain didn't know any other way. I had already surrendered, but before I could turn things around I continued to go through the motions of one more fall.

Less than twenty-four hours after returning from Orlando, Gibson and I were back where we'd started—broke, dope-sick, and desperate for cash. Gibson had disappeared hours earlier in an endless pursuit of crack. Meanwhile, I still had some stolen jewelry, tools, clothing, and other odds and ends we'd nicked, and I needed to figure out how to pawn them. I knew the jewelry was my best bet. On the streets even kitschy costume junk moves fast, and I had a couple of bags of big gaudy necklaces, brooches, and dangling earrings made of metal and glass. I collected my stuff and slowly opened the door, careful to look both ways. Instead of checking for cars before crossing a street, I was doing a visual sweep for cops before leaving our motel room.

It had been hours since my last fix and the tweak was in full effect, following my every move. I needed to walk around and get out of my head.

I made my way down the street, past the cast of sketchy characters who inhabited the Florida night, until I reached the gas station. This was a favored harbor for derelicts, addicts, oddballs, and a group of teenagers who regularly loitered out front listening to music on their stolen iPods. The gas pumps, partially sheltered under a pavilion of cracked plastic and shorting fluorescent lights, never seemed to be working. The station owner, a squat Indian guy with a thick, neatly trimmed beard, was always calling the cops. They'd sweep in, bust up the crowd, and leave, but like clockwork everyone would come back as soon as the cops were gone.

My usual routine consisted of panhandling or talking to random strangers, basically doing anything to rustle up a couple of bucks. I spent hours sweating people for loose change or odd dollar bills that I could combine to buy a bag of crack. Over time I had become an expert at reading people. I was a cognitive contortionist, concocting a story that I somehow sensed would earn me sympathy with whoever I was talking to. On a typical night I'd come up with ten different versions of myself. To an overweight young woman, I was the gentleman, opening her car door for her and bombarding her with compliments that I hoped she would exchange for a few bucks and a hot meal. Other times I'd hone in on a soccer mom, telling her a heartbreaking tale of my abusive father who spent his days beating the crap out of my helpless mother and me. For a trusting old lady, I'd go into high gear, often overplaying the sympathy card. "I was thrown out of my house with just the clothes on my back," I'd say. "If you could just give me twenty dollars for a train ticket to my aunt's place in Orlando, I'd be forever grateful."

Like a falcon searching the sky for pigeons, I assiduously surveyed my surroundings, waiting patiently as I looked for an opportunity to swoop in on that one vulnerable person who seemed ripe for the taking. All I needed was one. Getting at least one person to listen took work, but I always managed to grab someone's attention. While being a white, Jewish boy from a nice neighborhood made me stand out with dealers, here it was an asset. People tended to trust me, and cops didn't give me a second glance because I was such a "nice-looking" boy.

This wasn't my night. Hours passed and I had nothing. Now the station was strangely deserted except for one old black guy who had taken up residence on a metal newspaper rack in front of the convenience store window. I guessed that he was about seventy, tall and thin, wearing untied, tattered yellow construction boots that nearly engulfed his lower legs. His close-cropped hair tapered into an unkempt, blazing white beard that contrasted exquisitely with his dark skin. It was late. He wanted something. No one came to that gas station to fill their tank.

"What's in the bag?" he blurted out in a raspy voice that sounded like he'd consumed way too much alcohol. I didn't answer, but he motioned for me to follow him anyway. I had nothing to lose. With my bag of jewelry in hand, I followed him north from the gas station, past an unbroken stream of graffiti-covered walls, liquor stores, pawnshops, and run-down bodegas. After a while, I turned back and watched the

Fort Lauderdale skyline as the last sliver of civilization faded from view and pieces of Martin Luther King Boulevard started falling into place.

This was an area of Fort Lauderdale that even the cops avoided. Dealers and hookers carried out their business here in broad daylight. At night, a cacophony of gunshots, sirens, helicopters, and anguished screams rang through the streets like some sick ghetto lullaby. The last time I'd been here I saw a tall muscular guy with a massive scar on his left cheek pounding the crap out of some poor woman, a crack whore probably. She just lay there in the fetal position, letting out agonizing groans as he punched and kicked her again and again. But I needed to be here. This was South Florida crack central.

Another hour passed. I was still trailing the old black guy. By now I was getting desperate to get out of there, but I had to see this through. I was exhausted and utterly dope-sick. I needed drugs, and I needed them now. We walked a few more blocks before hooking up with a guy who ran a small but profitable after-hours business trafficking stolen goods from a window on the side of his house. The funny thing was, the house looked perfectly normal. There were toys, soccer balls, and a little red tricycle in the front yard. But if you walked to the side of the house and knocked on the window in a certain way at a certain time of day, the guy would answer. Everything was done in code, and it was clear that the old guy had been here before.

I'd come across a lot of guys like this over the years. I'm not proud of it, but stealing was my thing when I was on the streets. It's how I survived. Besides taking things from people's cars, Gibson and I would go to trailer parks, bust in, and tear an air conditioning unit out of the wall. Then we sold it for fifty bucks. Other times I set my sights on retail stores with outdoor displays that ran on the honor system. There I found high-end saw blades, nuts, bolts, dimmer switches, and copper piping. I must have filched thousands of dollars' worth of stuff from those displays. Security was nonexistent back then. I even lifted tools that I then used to commit other crimes. Large flathead screwdrivers and heavy mallets were perfect for breaking into those huge lockboxes we found in the back of pickup trucks belonging to contractors. They were always filled with expensive equipment. Contractors are tough guys, but we grabbed their stuff without batting an eyelash. The going rate when selling this shit was $30 for a $500 saw. It wasn't fair, but to us $30 for an hour's worth of escape was a good deal.

The old guy took the bag of jewelry from me and walked to the side of the house, quickly disappearing from view. I didn't see the transaction go down, but I didn't care. By now, withdrawal symptoms were coming on in waves. Getting straight was my only thought. A crack hit would do the trick, take the edge off, and buy me some time until I could score more dope. After a few minutes of subdued haggling, the old guy came back with two crisp $10 bills in his hand. "Give me my fucking money," I said, but he shook his head. "We're going to split this shit," he told me. I wasn't in much of a position to argue.

The old guy knew I wanted crack; there was no other reason for me to be on MLK Boulevard. Flush with our $20, we made our way to a group of kids on bicycles. They were either dealers or lookouts, and young ones at that—ten, maybe twelve years old. Standing in the center of the crew was a tall, agonizingly thin kid who was a little older than the rest. He was dirty and smelled like spoiled milk, a crackhead for sure. Even among junkies, crackheads stand out. Meth leaves you toothless and psychotic; heroin dots your arms with abscesses and infections; weed just saps your motivation. But crack is a different animal. I've seen sane, stable lawyers and doctors give up everything—their families, friends, and careers—for crack. I never used another drug that plunged me down a hole after just the first use, not even heroin. The saying goes, "One hit is too many, a million ain't enough." If you use crack, it will eventually own you. I found it so addictive that I dreamed about getting high while I slept.

The old black guy opened his hand and produced one of our new tens. He handed it to the tall kid, stuffed the other in his pocket, and quickly bolted from the scene. I could tell he wasn't a base head. He just wanted a drink. The tall kid handed the money to a kid standing next to him, who gave him a fingernail-sized ball of crack in return. I stood on the sidelines, waiting for a chance to get in on the game. The whole thing went down as if I were invisible.

Suddenly, I realized these kids were ignoring me on purpose. The tall kid was planning to hoard the rock for himself. There was no way that was happening. I had just made everyone's dreams come true. The old man got his booze, this kid had the rock, and I had no more jewelry to sell, no money, and I needed a hit or I thought I'd die.

I wasn't looking to throw down with some crackhead and his posse of gun-toting buddies, but he had what I needed.

We started sizing each other up, trying to see what the other guy was going to do before making a move. Before long we were pushing and shoving, trying to gain the upper hand. I grabbed his shirt and threw him to the ground. Suddenly he pulled back, realizing I wasn't going to back down. He probably needed his fix as desperately as I did, and he knew there was no way he was escaping me to take a hit. He either had to share it with me or risk losing it all.

As we picked ourselves off the ground I felt a small trickle of blood moving down my pant leg. Bruises were already forming on my right forearm and shoulder. I took a deep breath and moved back a few steps, glancing at the other guy. There was a gaping hole in his right pant leg and a mixture of dirt and sweat covering his face. Looking at him, I realized he was probably only fifteen years old, but already his eyes were drawn and tired. "Let's just split this shit," he said. As he reached into his left pocket and pulled out a pipe my entire body sank with relief.

We each took a drag, inhaling fumes from a makeshift pipe fashioned out of a hollowed-out tire gauge fitted with a Brillo-pad filter. After just one hit, the rest of the gang suddenly jumped on my back and threw me to the ground, kicking and punching me nonstop. I felt my body starting to cave under the endless barrage of blows. Somehow I got off the pavement and scrambled away. They didn't chase me. They probably just wanted me out of their neighborhood. As a white boy in the ghetto, I was a lightning rod for cops. I looked around. The tall kid had vanished, and the crack had gone with him. That was it—five hours of hell for a single hit.

I made it around the block before I realized that I'd lost

my glasses at some point during the melee. With no other choice, I turned around and walked back to the scene with my face red and bloodied, my body aching and bruised, and my clothes ripped and caked with dirt. The kids were still there, and they immediately started hurling rocks at me, big ones. Out of the corner of my eye, I saw my glasses lying awkwardly in a small patch of grass. They were pretty beat-up, but I dodged the rocks as I ran over to fetch them.

As I walked back toward the gas station, the single crack hit had already worn off. But instead of tweaking, I just felt low-down and depressed. I already needed to get straight again, but I didn't have the strength to hustle or scam my way to the next score. I had already surrendered. I was done.

I don't know how long I was walking the streets when a cop drove by. As soon as he saw me walking away from the ghetto he flashed his lights and swerved in my direction. As he approached a hundred thoughts ran through my head. I knew I could just run; I'd done that plenty of times over the past few years, hiding in the bushes for hours until the cops disappeared. But this time was different. I didn't feel like running. Instead, I calmly sat down on the curb as the tall, clean-shaven cop got out of the car. He walked over and looked me right in the eye. "What were you doing in that neighborhood?"

"What the fuck do you think I was doing?"

"Open your hands," he ordered. My arms were pale, gaunt, and pocked with track marks. "You're in the wrong neighborhood for that," he said. Cops knew that MLK Boulevard was the place for crack, not heroin.

"I'm a junkie who likes to smoke crack," I told him.

"Now open your mouth." Suddenly there was a greater

force behind the cop's words. He searched my mouth for crack, but of course he found nothing. "Stand up and put your hands behind your back," he told me, but I already knew the drill.

When the cop asked for my name, I gave him the real one, adding, "There's definitely a warrant for my arrest." After confirming the warrant, the cop opened the door and sat me in the back of his squad car. I pressed my face against the window and watched my breath start to fog up the warm glass. Staring off into the night, I knew I was going to jail. But instead of being scared, I felt peaceful, almost relieved. It was finally over.

As I waited for the cop to process my information I asked him to turn on the car radio to 94.9 ZETA, an alternative rock station. Pearl Jam's "Alive" started blaring through the speakers. It was the first time I'd heard music in ages. Slowly, a Cheshire cat smile spread across my face. Despite knowing what was coming—that I'd be sick, confined to a cell, detoxing in the worst imaginable way—I felt giddy. The cop stared at me in the rearview mirror, puzzled. "What are you smiling about?" he asked.

"I'm going to get my life back," I told him. "I'm going to get my family back."

On the way to the station the cop grabbed a couple of other guys for drug possession and petty theft. It was a few hours before I ended up in the holding cell, pacing back and forth like a maniac. This was the worst part—the waiting—especially for an addict like me who can't sit still. I spent the entire night languishing in that cell, tormented by withdrawal symptoms, tweaking like mad, and constantly looking over my shoulder, before being transferred to Broward County Jail the next day. There were ten of us convicts seated in the back of that dirty, windowless van, shackled together like farm animals being carted off to a meatpacking plant.

Broward County Jail is an eight-story, maximum-security facility adjacent to the County Courthouse in downtown Fort Lauderdale. Most guys there are awaiting trial or sentencing. Some are serving twelve-month terms. Anyone with a longer sentence than twelve months is sent to a different facility. More than twelve months is "hard time," and that means prison.

During booking each of us was medically evaluated. Some guys were sent to the hospital before entering jail for gunshot or knife wounds. We were checked for tuberculosis, HIV, and other diseases associated with using. A nurse asked about drug use—what kinds of drugs I used, how often, and how recently I used them. I thought it should have been pretty obvious in my case. Sometimes, if they know you're using, you're put on "detox protocol," which includes checks from medical staff. But I was a junkie. Even though heroin withdrawal is considered a medical emergency, there was no protocol for me.

The first two weeks in jail were torture. It was so overcrowded that they didn't even have a cell for me. I sat stewing in a cold, windowless concrete box with no comfort except for a dirty mattress on the floor. I was on the first floor, which was general population—mixed together were dealers, addicts, rapists, and murderers. As withdrawal took hold I suffered through anxiety, psychotic thoughts, and panic attacks. Then every inch of my body started to ache. Diarrhea, nausea, mind-numbing back pain, achy bones, and profuse sweating were followed by profound cold. I felt like I was going to die. Some jails treat junkies with methadone or clonidine, which calms the nerves, but since there was a month before my sentencing I got shit, just a handful of Imodium and ibuprofen every six hours. I couldn't eat for weeks. Every day another inmate stole my lunch, but I didn't have the energy or appetite to fight for it.

The physical withdrawal took a few weeks to subside. By then I was moved up to the fourth floor, which was marginally better. I started eating, mostly carbohydrates, since that's what they served us. In just a few weeks I gained over thirty pounds. Then I started having vivid, graphic dreams about scoring, looking for drugs, and getting high. I woke up every morning exhausted, as if I hadn't slept at all.

By the time I got a court date my physical detox was mostly over. I called Sam, who I counted on to be there for me despite the many ways I'd fucked up over the years. His friendship was, and still is, one of the greatest gifts of my life. Sam spoke to several of my family members and finally got the name of a family friend, Cindy, who was a public defender. But I was scheduled to appear in court the following day, and there was no time to reach her. My only option was a court-appointed public defender.

For my first court appearance, I was roused at 5:00 A.M. and chain-linked to other inmates awaiting sentencing before being transferred to the courthouse. It was a humiliating, dehumanizing experience. After arriving in court, I walked up a long flight of stairs before being escorted, still in handcuffs, into the courtroom. From there I was seated in the jury box and had to wait for my name to be called. Minutes before I was set to appear, my court-appointed attorney ambled over to me. He was stone-faced and grim and clearly saw me as yet another run-of-the-mill junkie.

"Jesse," he told me, "I have to be honest. If you're lucky, you'll get five years in jail." My heart started racing, and suddenly I couldn't breathe. I asked him, "Can we postpone the hearing until I get in touch with Cindy?" He walked back to the county prosecutor, and he agreed. For the next five hours I sat in that jury box, alone with my thoughts, unable to leave until each prisoner had appeared before the judge.

I thought that Cindy would have better news, but the picture seemed equally bleak when I spoke to her the next day. "You violated your probation," she told me. "Bail isn't an option. But I can get you out on house arrest." The problem was, I didn't have a house. I had no money and nowhere to go. I knew my family wanted nothing to do with me.

"I think I'll just stew in jail for a while," I told her. "My plan is long-term treatment." She advised me to apply for a transfer to the rehab program at Conte Facility, another Broward County jail. There I would at least get the help I needed.

There was another month until my sentencing, though, and I spent it back in jail. In many ways, it was a good thing that I had been on the streets because I learned some things there that ended up saving my ass in jail. The main lesson was, if it's not yours, don't touch it, and if it's none of your business, don't go near it. Luckily, I knew how to keep to myself, and I quickly learned the strange unwritten rules of jail—like to always spit in the toilet instead of the sink, to get up and walk around the table if you needed something instead of reaching over another inmate, and most important, to never change the channel on the TV. One time several weeks into my sentence another guy was flipping through the channels and passed the Food Network. I caught a glimpse of Rachael Ray. My passion for food had been completely taken over by my addiction, but there was still a spark within me, a deep fascination that struggled to get out. Now that I was clean, I felt it rising. At that point I was desperate to watch anything related to food, but all the other guys wanted to watch *Jerry Springer,* and I knew that if I changed the channel I'd get hurt.

I was back in court a month later, and this time Cindy and I went before the judge. We had already reached a deal with the prosecuting attorney, so I knew what was coming. Six months in county jail followed by six months in a state-run therapeutic community, three months in a halfway house, and then two years' probation. I heaved a sigh of relief. It felt good knowing I would have a place to stay and dry out. After more than a year on the streets, I would get three meals a day, medical care, and a roof over my head. No more sleeping in dirty alleyways. No more waking up to hundreds of mosquito bites. No more need to scam or hustle unwitting strangers for a couple of dollars. Jail was the best place for me at that moment. I could finally let go of the scamming, hustling, and lying and figure out where to go from here.

Back at jail, I exchanged my white wristband for a yellow one, indicating that I had been sentenced. It was a small change, but I saw it as a symbolic one. Finally, I was on my way.

CHAPTER TEN

Dry-Aged

Dry-aged: Beef that has been hung or placed on a rack for several weeks to dry.

In October 2003 I was halfway through my six-month stint in jail when word came down that I was being transferred to Conte, an intensive substance abuse program within another jail. I was ready. My physical addiction had long passed, and the dreams were gone too. For two months I had woken up to intense, vivid recollections of a belt tightening around my forearm or a needle slowly penetrating my skin. There's a beginning, middle, and end to physical addiction, and I'd made it through all of them for what I knew would be the last time. But the craving, the mental addiction, hadn't yet subsided.

At Conte I was assigned to a cell with a guy named Louie as my roommate. He was doing time for possession of crack, a class A misdemeanor that carries a one-year minimum sentence. He was forty and had been in and out of the system since he was fifteen. Louie was a big boy—at least six-three and fucking ripped. When he talked, his neck muscles twitched, especially if he was excited, and the scars above his left eyebrow and across his chin cemented his reputation as someone to never fuck with.

The cell I shared with Louie had a toilet, a sink, a bunk bed, and a little area for our possessions. The walls were bare. Displaying personal artifacts was not allowed. Since this was jail, not prison, the inmates carried short-term sentences and there were no bars on the cells, just a large Plexiglas window and door that made a loud suctioning sound when closed.

By then Louie knew the ropes. Jail was his second home. "I live better in the jail than I do on the streets," he once told me, and I could see why. People feared and therefore respected him, and he was like the mayor of Conte. Having a good "cellie" is key when doing time, and I was lucky to have Louie as mine. We hit it off immediately, united in part by a shared addiction to crack.

Jail was a little city of its own with its own rules of engagement, separate from the outside world. Survival was all about relationships, and the interactions between guards and prisoners were an important dynamic. Some guards and inmates had an "us versus them" mentality and drew a line in the sand: the guards viewed the inmates as something less than human, and the inmates saw the guards as the enemy. I had a different way of looking at it, figuring that it couldn't hurt to get in tight with the guards. One of them, Tom, worked the graveyard shift. He was a nice guy, tall and lanky, with the standard-issue buzz cut. Like me, Tom hailed from Parkland and had a family member who was a junkie, so we shared an immediate connection.

It was the prisoners' job to clean the facility. Guards woke some guys up in the middle of the night to help scrub the toilets, mop floors, or do whatever else needed to get done. Believe it or not, this was a coveted gig. To an inmate, any time spent outside of a cell is time well spent. Two or three nights a week, Tom got me out of my bunk. I'd use a huge machine and spend hours polishing the floors. Then Tom would walk me to the staff lounge for a reward of Cheetos, potato chips, and even caffeinated coffee.

In the mornings we went to group therapy, and in the afternoons we attended Alcoholics Anonymous or Narcotics Anonymous meetings that were held in the jail by a group called Hospitals and Institutions. They traveled around, bringing meetings to people who couldn't get out to them. I knew the guys from Hospitals and Institutions from my time at BARC and all the other rehabs I'd been in before. Back then, everything they said had sounded like gibberish to me. I just didn't care. I said the right things and temporarily modified my behavior, but inside I was the same depraved human being. I didn't pay attention to the significance of the twelve steps—sharing, making amends, admitting powerlessness, and whatever other bullshit they were peddling. At least, that's how I saw it at the time. I heard the words, but I didn't listen to the message. It went in one ear and out the other.

But now I was dry and sober for the longest time since I was twelve years old, and something was different. I had been beaten down so low that I knew the only way was up from here, and I was finally willing to do whatever it took to get there. In the past I'd sat in those meetings silently judging the crackheads around me, only half-listening to what they were saying. But now I heard the guys from Hospitals and Institutions say, "I'm thirty years sober. I made it. You can too," and suddenly I believed them. I listened, really listened to their stories, and realized that their stories were my story too. My judgment washed away, and I embraced the other addicts as it hit me for the first time that I was truly one of them.

Another guy said, "I lost my job, my family, everything. For ten years, I stole from and lied to everyone I met, including my wife and parents, but somehow I got it all back." I got goose bumps. I was so determined not to live the same way anymore that I was drawing at straws for serenity, and these words inspired me, instilling faith in a higher power that I had never believed in before. My family wasn't religious. We celebrated the cultural aspects of Judaism, but we never talked about God. But the people right in front of me clearly got so much joy from their faith that I started to believe too—not in the God from the Bible, but a God of my own understanding. I became not religious exactly, but deeply spiritual, and it slowly dawned on me that getting arrested the day after falling to my knees and surrendering had been no coincidence. God had picked me up out of that sludge of misery, I realized, and every time I felt a connection to someone's story, I knew it was the work of God.

Sitting in those meetings, I could feel the desire to get high lift off me and drift away. There's a saying, "When the student is ready, the teacher appears," and as my physical cravings for drugs faded my teacher appeared. The twelve steps talk about handing over our will and our lives to a higher power that can restore us to sanity, and in jail I gladly surrendered my will to God. I was so beaten down by my experiences on the street that I was wide open and willing, and it felt good to sit back and let someone else think for me. For the first time in years I wasn't standing in a river trying to walk upstream, and I experienced an entirely new feeling—peace.

After a month I heard that a couple of guys a few cells down from me got picked up at eleven each night and came back in the morning. I asked Louie where they went. "Kitchen detail," he told me. My immediate response was, "I've got to get on that detail." I talked to Tom, and eventually I was able to join the kitchen crew. We worked the Bravo shift—midnight to 5:00 A.M. Lights out was at 9:00 P.M., and I didn't get picked up until 11:00, so I just killed time for two hours, waiting to get into the kitchen.

About a half hour before pickup, the guys on kitchen detail lined up and were chain-linked together. From there it was a short drive to the commissary kitchen, which was in a long white building between Conte and the women's house. That kitchen was like nothing I had ever seen before. The refrigerator had enough space for at least fifty long racks; the oven was a huge walk-in. There was a twenty-foot-long stainless steel table we used as an assembly line to make sandwiches. But when I got there, it was a fucking mess. Next to the table was a ten-foot-tall rack full of cheap white bread wrapped in plastic. Half of the guys started by grabbing the bread and slapping on a piece of mystery meat. Then they handed it to the next guy, who had no idea what to do with it. The whole thing was totally unorganized, and it drove me crazy. Eventually I put some order to the process, giving each guy on the line a specific job and turning it into a functioning assembly line.

My job was to make the mashed potatoes, and we went through hundreds of pounds of instant potatoes a day, cooking them in kettles that would hold three bodies. Every Sunday we made chicken, placing the chicken legs on sheet pans and pushing them into the huge walk-in oven. From there, we put the food into huge hotel pans that were placed in transfer containers and taken to each cell block.

There was almost no room for creativity when cooking this unadorned, mass-produced food. Spices, even salt, were strictly forbidden. But I still put maximum effort into everything I was doing. Some inmates didn't like working in the kitchen. It was a lot of work to prepare food for hundreds of inmates and the entire staff, plus we had to clean up before finishing our shift. Others found it demoralizing to serve the same guys we were doing time with, but this didn't make sense to me. The fact is, we were all doing time. I didn't think it could get any more demoralizing than that.

To me, the commissary kitchen was like a slice of heaven in jail. During my shift there were two guards present and five inmates with 20,000 square feet of kitchen space to work in. During the day guards would get pissed if an inmate left the cafeteria with an extra piece of bread or fruit, but us guys who worked the kitchen left our shift with half of the fucking refrigerator tucked under our shirts.

Of course not everything was fun and games. The guys were always fucking with each other, doing anything they could to gain the upper hand. Early on Louie told me,

"You've got to set a precedent. Don't show any weakness. If some guy fucks with you or even looks at you the wrong way, you have to hit him." These were wise words that eventually came in handy.

Jerry and I had a couple of run-ins. He was doing a year for selling, and in jail word got around fast. I heard some whispers and knew he'd been talking shit about me. The other guys were wondering why I hadn't responded, and eventually I knew they would start thinking I was a punk. I couldn't let Jerry get away with it. I had to set a precedent.

One night I saw Jerry waiting in line for dinner. I walked over, placed my hands on his shoulders, and shoved him aside, taking his spot. "Fucking cracker-ass bitch," he said. "Who do you think you are?" I didn't say anything, but my body language clearly stated, *I'm the motherfucker who just took your place in line. What are you gonna do about it?* Jerry puffed out his chest and then lunged in my direction with his fists clenched and his eyes full of rage. I was ready—I didn't flinch. The guards were watching, and they grabbed Jerry before anything else could happen. For the moment, it was over.

A few mornings later it was the end of my shift at 5:00 A.M. It had been a long night making over 500 sandwiches. I walked over to the sink to wash my hands before exiting the kitchen, and as I rounded the corner I suddenly fell to the floor, the full weight of my body landing squarely on my left knee. I could see a trickle of blood seeping through a tear in my pants. Behind me I heard laughter. I knew that voice. I picked myself off the ground, and there was Jerry, standing just a few feet away. He was pointing in my direction and still laughing.

I knew what I had to do. I stood up, adrenaline pumping, ready to beat the shit out of this guy, when the guard suddenly yelled, "Line up!" It was time for the nightly strip search before being transported back to the main facility. Thankfully, these searches weren't very thorough, or we would never have gotten away with pilfering as much food from the kitchen as we did.

Once I got back to my cell, Louie started asking about my torn pants. "Fucking Jerry" was all I could say.

"Man, I told you," he said. "You gotta send a message. Can't let anyone get over on you like that. Don't worry. My boys will take care of it." These were the same guys who had first turned me on to the kitchen detail. We walked over to their cell and told them about the situation with Jerry.

"Meet us at the walk-in tonight at three sharp," they said.

I approached the refrigerator later that night. From behind the door I heard a loud crashing sound that I knew was Jerry. When I walked in, he was lying on the floor with his head covered by a sheet pan. Louie's two guys were holding him down. One of the guys looked up at me, but no one said a word. They didn't have to. I knew what I had to do.

In jail everyone talks like he's a tough guy. I constantly heard other inmates claiming, "I'll kick his ass," but none of them ever threw a punch. I wasn't a violent person; I'd ended up there because I was an addict. And facing the moment where I had to take action as a means of survival was scary. But I couldn't let the other guys see that I was afraid, so I dropped to the floor, removed the sheet pan, and started punching Jerry in the face. Jerry let out a gut-wrenching howl, like the cry of a wounded animal. His right eye started swelling shut as blood poured from both of his nostrils.

I felt awful. I wanted to stop, but I knew I couldn't. Sweat collected on my brow and my glasses slipped, dropping down to the tip of my nose. Soon I felt adrenaline coursing through my body, and as I hit Jerry again and again, the fear I had felt gave way to a strange sense of satisfaction, like every punch was releasing years' worth of pent-up anger. In an instant, it all came flooding back—the resentment I had built up toward my parents, the months of sleeping on cardboard boxes and scrounging through Dumpsters looking for something to eat, the entire reality of my debauched, drug-fueled existence. Finally I had exhausted myself, and the guilt and shame returned immediately. I got up. "Don't fuck with me ever again," I told Jerry, standing over him.

He never did. And after the other guys saw what had happened to Jerry, no one else did either. I had earned my stripes.

When we lined up to go back to the main facility, it was obvious that Jerry had been jumped. "What happened to your face, Jerry?" the guard asked.

"I fell," Jerry said. "It's nothing."

"So be it." The guard turned to the group. "No one is going to tell me what happened to Jerry?" His question was met with silence. "Then you're all staying an extra hour to scrub pots."

In jail you never rat. The beating Jerry got from me was like a butterfly kiss compared to what would have happened to him—or any of the guys—if they had ratted.

At Conte it was rise and shine at 7:00 A.M. sharp, but anyone who worked the kitchen graveyard shift could crash until 10:00. Getting up always sucked. I didn't have any commissary money, and the only people who ever came to visit me were Grandpa Seymour and Grandma Audrey and my friend Sam. One day I got a letter from Grandpa Laz saying that he believed in me and loved me, and I held it tight, believing that if I worked the program and lived with integrity I could get my family back.

Other guys used their commissary money to buy cookies, radios, and whatever the hell else they wanted. I became industrious and started doing little things in exchange for these goodies. I offered to fold the other inmates' laundry for a cup of soup or some Snickers bars. Or during my shift in the kitchen I'd snatch a pair of latex gloves, snip off the fingers, and fill them with salt. I'd stick them in my shoe or hide them in my armpit. Salt was always a hot commodity. After months of eating bland, tasteless food, a little bit could go a long way.

It wasn't long before I found other uses for those latex gloves. "Fifis," or makeshift vaginas made of latex gloves, were very popular among the inmates. Even a man in jail needs some loving. I had several Fifis and even gave them their own names. Delores was a good one, but when she popped on me one time when I was fucking her, it was over between us. When I didn't have a Fifi, I just made do with porn. Guys circulated magazines around. Sometimes I cut out a picture and stuck it to a wet tile in the shower. Other times I took a picture of a naked woman and laid it down next to a pillow while I was going at it with my Fifi.

The commissary kitchen was really two kitchens—one for the inmates and one for the staff. In the walk-in refrigerator there were shelves stacked with cold cuts and meat. Obviously these items were strictly off-limits for inmates. One day I noticed a large pork shoulder. It must have weighed fifteen pounds, swaddled in fat and collagen. My mouth started watering. I knew that when the pork was cooked, the fat would melt away, leaving the meat moist and tender. The collagen would break down into simple sugars, giving the meat a sweet, juicy taste. I couldn't stop thinking about that pork. At night I dreamed about eating it with my bare hands, the juices running down my face. I showed it to the other guys, and I could see them salivating. We made a pact to take the pork and share it if an opportunity arose.

Before long a moment came along when no one was looking. I quickly stuffed the pork shoulder under an apron and placed it in a box with some other items. Then I went about my business. There was a row of stack ovens in the kitchen, and I surreptitiously covered one of the red oven lights with black tape so the guards wouldn't know it was in use. Then I had the other inmates form a line in front of me. There wasn't much time. Quickly I threw the pork shoulder in a bowl and marinated it with a dry rub of pilfered garlic powder, onion powder, salt, and oregano—basically anything I could get my hands on. Then I placed it on a baking tray and slid it into the oven, closing the door gently. Then we all got back to making sandwiches. The guards had no clue what we were doing.

It took four hours for the shoulder to cook through. Quietly, I opened the oven door and paused for just a brief moment, savoring the aroma of the freshly cooked meat. The other inmates and I took turns tearing off pieces to eat. The pork was perfectly cooked, succulent and juicy. It had been months since I'd eaten any flavored food, and years since I had enjoyed any food without pills, heroin, or crack dulling my senses. I relished every bite.

At the end of our shift we took what was left of our prize, wrapped it in tinfoil, and hid it on a shelf behind rows of tomato paste and chickpeas. We munched on it for two days until it went bad. It was a risk taking that pork shoulder, but it was worth it. For me, the reward wasn't just the satisfaction of eating it, but the ability to really cook and eat for the first time in years as a sober person. My passion for food had never gone away, but it had been sundered by years of addiction and abuse. It felt strange to reconnect with this intrinsic part of myself in the most depressing and unlikely of settings. Now my love for food had returned in the same pure, unfiltered form I had previously only experienced as a child. I was grateful to have it back under any circumstances. I knew if I could harness that passion, I could use it to make the culinary world my oyster.

CHAPTER ELEVEN

Aperitif

Aperitif: An alcoholic beverage that is usually dry rather than sweet and is often served before a meal to stimulate the appetite.

Schenker, pack it up."

I knew this day was coming. My six-month sentence was up. But instead of being elated, I didn't want to leave Conte, where I was safe. Before going to jail I had been high or strung out ever since I was a child. I didn't know the first thing about how to take care of myself.

I gathered my few possessions and hugged my cellie Louie. Then it was time to go. Accompanied by two guards, I walked the short distance to a filthy holding cell in the main jail, the final stop before release. It was then about a half hour's drive in a sheriff's van to Turning Point Bridge Work Release, a state-run therapeutic community. This would be my first step before either reentering the real world or, if I fucked up, making a short trip back to jail.

The "smoke pit" at Turning Point was a small grassy area out front surrounded by a thick layer of brown mulch. Everything else was covered in gray asphalt and brick. In rainy weather the pit turned brown and discarded cigarette butts floated in the puddles of mud. The rules at Turning Point were strict. It wasn't jail, but it was no country club either. The atmosphere was highly structured, and the punishments frequently excessive. If you lit up outside the pit, you'd get a violation. Three violations meant a DR, or disciplinary write-up. Three DRs was all it took to go back to jail.

Upon entering Turning Point, I had little contact with the outside world. That had to be earned. It was like a work camp, and I spent all day at the facility sweeping leaves from the front porch, scrubbing floors on my hands and knees, folding laundry, attending meetings, being screamed at, or watching the cops tackle other residents and haul them back to jail. There was a hierarchy among the residents, and we monitored each other. A resident who had earned conferred status for good behavior could dress another resident down for the smallest bullshit, like making a five-inch lengthwise pleat on his bed instead of a six-inch pleat. If a guy screwed up or slacked off, he would get paraded around the grounds with a sign detailing his transgressions. There was no such thing as privacy. We all showered together in a large, open room. The bathroom had no stalls, just one long row of toilets. Even in jail the bathrooms had stalls.

There were therapists, counselors, orderlies, and even a doctor on site. Prior to being admitted, all residents were tested for TB and HIV, and as soon as I arrived they also ran my blood work. When the results came in, my liver function was sky-high. "Your test results indicate that you most likely have hepatitis C," the doctor told me without looking me in the eye. "Fortunately, it's treatable."

Later when I was released from Turning Point and was able to get a proper physical, I learned that I never had hepatitis C. Turing Point hadn't done a conclusive test; they just made an assumption when my liver function came back high. But I didn't know this at the time, and I walked back to the smoke pit and sat on the edge of a bench, not knowing what to do with this information. My palms grew moist and small beads of perspiration formed around my lips as I took a long, slow drag from a Camel. My legs began to twitch, and I could feel my anxiety level rising, but this was completely different from the sense of unease I'd experienced before. In the past, my anxiety came on suddenly and then disappeared just as quickly. I could never pinpoint its source. But this time the anxiety had a specific object to latch on to—fear. There was no escaping it; drugs were not an option. For the first time in my life I knew, clean and sober, what it meant to be afraid.

Ms. Schumacher, my therapist at Turning Point, was a take-no-bullshit chick with thick-framed, oversized glasses, a discordant mop of blond hair that moved in multiple directions even when she was sitting down, and a noticeable limp. Her accent was Deep South all the way, probably from North Florida, Georgia, or Alabama. At our first meeting I sat down on the couch in her institutional white office. The walls were empty except for a lone painting of sailboats and a freebie calendar opened to the wrong month. On top of her desk sat stacks of files and an old-school Rolodex. She pulled up a chair and peered at me through those glasses. "You like heroin, don't cha?"

She sure didn't waste any time. "What the fuck?" I said in response.

"I've seen enough of you boys to know who likes to go up and who likes to go down," she told me. "You got a relaxed look about ya." No one had ever told me I looked "relaxed" before, but Ms. Schumacher got me right away.

Over the next month we talked every day about my life, my family, my drug use, my goals, and my plans for the future. I dove into meetings and therapy at Turning Point. My intentions were good, and I was aligned with my higher power, and I felt like nothing could fucking stop me. I was invincible. In recovery I was finally learning a way to live that didn't agitate me. By now I knew that, as an addict, I couldn't let myself get too down or too up—that was when things got wavy. I figured out how to live in the middle, making up rules to keep myself at bay, to avoid too much intense feeling. This allowed me to get out of my own way, but by avoiding emotions I still never learned how to process them in a healthy way.

As I talked to Ms. Schumacher my psychology started catching up with my biology. For years I had been stunting my emotional growth with drugs; by the time I got to Turning Point I was twenty-one but emotionally only about thirteen. Slowly everything started to catch up, and after two months I was emotionally fifteen. Month after month of meetings, structure, and therapy helped me finally catch up to my chronological age. I had been clean for only six months, but I was already a changed man, living in the moment and full of gratitude just to be alive.

One day Ms. Schumacher said out of nowhere, "Now, tell me about the watch." I had never mentioned a word about the watch during our sessions. I never told anyone else about it either. How did she know about that fucking watch? But it didn't matter. Her simple question opened the floodgates, and I told her how stealing my mother's Rolex was the breaking point that ended my relationship with my family.

Our visitors at Turning Point were carefully screened—not that it mattered much in my case. No one really came to see me except for Sam. He swung by once a week with clothes and food. I had gone straight from the streets to jail, so I didn't have any clothes of my own when I got to Turning Point. Sam went to a Walmart and bought me a few outfits, a pair of shoes, and some underwear so at least I had something to wear. Sometimes he gave me a few dollars so I could buy soda from the vending machine. But one morning he came by unexpected. He didn't have any food or clothes with him. "Let's go for a walk," he said, and as we stood outside Sam didn't waste any time. "Your parents are ready to see you," he told me.

I didn't know what to say. I didn't even know what to think. For over two years I'd had no idea what my family was doing or what they even thought about me. Sam said, "I think they were happy to learn that you were still alive." As he continued talking I thought about the prospect of reuniting with my family. How would I be able to excuse or explain all the harm I had caused and the misery I'd inflicted? When I left, we were a fractured, broken family. Had anything changed?

But instead of feeling angst about a possible reunion, I was at peace with it. I had already surrendered my will and felt so accepting of everything that I didn't have any expectations. I was free. I believed in my higher power and knew that a reunion would happen when it was right.

Ms. Schumacher spoke to my parents over the phone and with me in our regular sessions. Finally she suggested a meeting in the staff lounge at Turning Point. I was still nervous, but I figured if Ms. Schumacher thought I was ready, then I was ready. My parents arrived before me and spoke first to Ms. Schumacher. Then I went in. I felt anxious, but also confident that I wasn't the same person as the Jesse they had last seen. I was reuniting with my parents as a completely different person.

As I walked down the hallways toward the lounge I saw a group of residents milling about. Through an open window I caught a glimpse of my family talking with Ms. Schumacher. Even from a distance, I could feel their anxiety. I felt for them in that moment. They had no idea what I would be like or how this would all play out.

I walked right up to my mother and buried my head deep in her chest. "Call me Jesse Blake," I said, my tears wetting her shirt. She was one of the only people in the world who called me by my middle name. My father and Joee closed their arms around us, and we all cried together as we embraced in silence.

After a while we sat down, and one after the other my father, mother, and sister shared their anger and hurt. My parents told me how relieved they were when Sam told them I'd been arrested. Before that, every night they'd listened in fear for the phone to ring with the news that I was dead. My sister told me that after I left she was so devastated that she couldn't eat. I had really fucked up her world. For once, as I listened, I was completely genuine. I didn't feel like I had to talk a lot or manipulate anything. Instead, I listened to everything they said, and then I apologized, taking full ownership of my behavior. For the first time in my life I didn't defend myself to them or concoct any wild stories. "I'm clean just for today," I told them.

I saw my parents again once I earned the right for a leave from Turning Point. They picked me up on a Sunday afternoon. As we pulled up to my childhood home I asked my parents to stop at the end of the driveway so I could bring the empty trash cans up to the garage. I wanted to show them that I was different, that things would be different from now on. While I was there, I made sure to never be out of their sight. I even asked for their permission to use the bathroom. When we talked, they wanted to know where I had been and what I had gone through. It was uncomfortable for me to talk about this, but Ms. Schumacher had told me that I needed to say it and they needed to hear it, so the truth came out little by little.

The only thing I was afraid of then was that the allergy, the desire to get high, would return. Every inch of my parents' house served as a reminder of the things I had said or done in the past to get high. But instead of dragging me back there, being home only motivated me even more to push forward with integrity. In therapy I had learned to take my parents off the pedestal and stop expecting them to be perfect. They were human and had their own baggage, just like everyone else, but they loved me and had done their best to give me a good life. Most important, I'd stopped worrying about how I fit into their belief system and started focusing on doing the right things for me.

By month four at Turning Point, I finally earned the right to look for a job off the grounds. I got a bus card and headed straight to Big City Tavern on Las Olas Boulevard. Big City Tavern was one of Broward County's better-known restaurants. I spoke with Jeff Haskell, the executive chef there, explaining that I was in work release at Turning Point. "Be here at nine tomorrow," he said.

The next morning I showed up at 7:00. It was Jeff's day off, so I was working with the sous chef, Jared. First we toured the kitchen. "This is your station," Jared said, pointing to the restaurant's massive grill. Every day from 11:00 A.M. to 3:00 P.M. the orders poured in, sandwich after sandwich of chicken, burgers, and fish. On most days we did 300 covers. There was a printer above my station, and every time an order came in I ripped off the check and put it on the rail. But eventually I got so busy that I stopped looking at the checks to see what the customers had ordered. I just started piling salmon, hamburgers, and chicken breasts on the grill, figuring I'd be right more often than not. If I just kept firing food, I knew that eventually I would need whatever I was putting on the grill. Over time I learned that grill like it was the back of my hand. The right side got really hot, so I put things there that I wanted to char or crisp. The middle of the grill was slightly cooler, so I used it to toast buns and put things there if I didn't want them to cook through.

After work, my apron was always covered in a mixture of sweat and seasoning. I looked down at the printer paper collecting on the floor. Over the course of my shift, the entire roll had printed out, stretching out over 250 feet to the kitchen's back door. Soon I picked up a couple of night shifts, which were even crazier. From 5:00 to 10:00 P.M. the grill got hammered with orders for filet mignon, strip steaks, and trout. My complete and utter focus in the kitchen had returned. The orders kept coming in, and I found immense satisfaction in turning them out one after the other. This quickly became my new high.

Thanks in part to my busy schedule of work and therapy, my six months at Turning Point passed quickly. After "graduating," I moved into a halfway house on Federal Highway with fifteen other recovering addicts. I remained focused, working all day and attending meetings at night. Once a month I checked in with my probation officer and took a urine test, and in between my probation officer popped in unannounced to check up on me at work or at the halfway house. I was very careful. Other cooks offered me a ride to or from work, but I always said no. I didn't know what was in their pockets, and if I was caught in a car with someone carrying drugs, I knew I'd get arrested for breaking my probation. My caution paid off. After a year my probation was terminated early for good behavior.

At this point my parents still weren't really involved in my life, but we saw each other occasionally and talked on the phone. I was very careful with them, always walking on eggshells, because I didn't want to say anything that would ruin the relationships we were just starting to rebuild. Soon I found that it was good to spend time together so they could see firsthand how I was living, rather than having to take my word for it when I told them about it over the phone. In the past I had always used words to manipulate my family, and I didn't want to risk them thinking that I was going down that road again. I wanted to show them my integrity with actions rather than words.

I worked up the nerve to invite my family to dinner at Big City, figuring that seeing me in my element was the best way for them to know how I was doing. When they agreed, I reserved the restaurant's nicest table and made sure we would be taken care of by our best server. I even bought a suit and tie. At dinner I didn't want to seem self-serving, so I asked about their lives, and when they asked me questions, I simply answered. It felt amazingly liberating to have nothing to hide or prove, and we were able to enjoy being together in a way we never could have in the past. I looked around the table and told them honestly, "I'm so grateful that we're all together again." At the end of the night I made sure to buy dinner, my way of showing them how determined I was to make my own way.

It had been so long since we had any semblance of a normal relationship; we were starting over from scratch. Slowly we built a new relationship. We started talking once a week, then twice a week. At first we saw each other once a month, and then it was twice a month, and then three times a month. Eventually we started to get comfortable around each other again, joking around and talking about music and sports like we used to. I was going to a lot of meetings, and they were attending Al-Anon meetings, so we had those new ways of connecting too. Just as I was really getting into food again and putting all of my energy and passion into building my career, little by little I got my family back.

My skills in the kitchen didn't go unnoticed by Chef Jeff or the partners of the Big City Restaurant Group, which owned several local restaurants. They were opening a new place in Coral Gables called City Cellar, which was basically an upscale wine bar. I was offered the position of sous chef. Now I was next in line after Jeff. Delegating was new for me, but it felt like a natural evolution. I was determined to lead by example, walking in every morning at seven and just going for it. No task was too menial. I cleaned the grill, scrubbed the walk-in, and even took out the garbage if I had to.

At City Cellar we made slightly more complicated dishes—Veal Scaloppine with Mushrooms, Grilled Lamb Shank with Parsnips, Glazed Duck Breast with Risotto, and Scallops with an Apricot Glaze. I did everything: flipping vegetables, throwing filets on the grill, tossing Caesar salads, and even pushing pizzas in the brick oven. On some nights Jeff and I knocked out 100 covers by ourselves while the other cooks just watched us in awe.

Jeff had every Sunday and Monday off, and on those days I was put in charge of the kitchen. Determined to kill it, I took advantage of my freedom in the kitchen by playing around with the specials, always pushing the envelope. One night I came up with a duck breast that was a play on saltimbocca. Instead of veal, I used duck that I pounded out thin, adding sage and a rich duck glaze. It was tender and delicious, and the customers loved it. I started experimenting with the polenta we served, rolling it out and mounting it with mushrooms and truffles before putting it in the fryer.

When I first started at Big City Grill, I kept to myself and focused solely on my work and recovery. It was my first real job in almost two years, and I was determined to do things right instead of being tempted by the other cooks' partying. But City Cellar was different. I was in charge. As I grew more secure in my role there and in my sobriety I built relationships with the other chefs. We shared war stories of our time in other kitchens.

I may have been clean, but my addictive behavior never went away. The longer I worked the program the more I was able to find a healthy outlet for my obsessiveness: food. I had started collecting restaurant menus as a kid, and now my collection had exploded into literally thousands of menus. In the kitchen I told the other chefs about the work Charlie Trotter and Thomas Keller were doing, along with a dozen other chefs I admired. Without drugs to spend my paychecks on, I bought cookbooks instead, devouring at least ten new cookbooks each week. My favorites were Andrew Dornenburg's masterful *Culinary Artistry;* Gray Kunz and Peter Kaminsky's *The Elements of Taste,* which redefines the idea of "taste" and gave me a whole new perspective on creating and characterizing food; Ferran Adrià's *El Bulli,* which raises cooking to an art form; Jacques Pepin's *La Technique,* which exquisitely but simply illuminates the fundamentals of cooking; and Michel Bras's *Essential Cuisine,* which sent my head spinning the first time I opened it.

Over time I built up a small library, and I studied these books the way a medical student pores over an anatomy text. The guys at the restaurant gave me shit for it, but I didn't care. I found the same peace within the pages of those cookbooks that I had first felt cutting vegetables at Nana Mae's feet.

When City Cellar had a new refrigerator delivered, it came in a huge wooden crate. The next day I came to work and found that Jeff had put a sign on the crate that read JESSE'S COOKBOOK COLLECTION—DON'T TOUCH.

Jeff may have made fun of my obsessiveness, but he saw that I wasn't talking out of my ass when it came to food. I was fast and skilled and, most important, passionate. The way he listened when I spoke and began to solicit my advice told me that I had earned his respect. Soon I could tell that we had crossed a new threshold in our relationship. We were no longer merely an employee and employer; we were colleagues.

Soon after starting at City Cellar, I moved out of the halfway house. I rented a beat-up studio in Miami in the back of a little house off Forty-Seventh Street. It was smack-dab in the middle of Little Haiti. Some of my neighbors had taken the entire backseat out of a Cadillac and placed it on the sidewalk in front of their home. They spent all day out there, playing dominoes. When I passed by, they offered me drugs. "No thanks," I told them. "I'm good." It may sound strange, but I loved that apartment and felt completely at home in that neighborhood. It kept me grounded and allowed me to keep to myself, which were both key to my recovery.

While I was living in Miami, I found out that my uncle Bruce in New Paltz had been diagnosed with stomach cancer. I flew up to see him in the hospital. Lying there, thin and pale, he told me how proud he was of me for getting clean. His death only a few months later was devastating. Thank God I was so involved in the program; I needed all of the support around me to come through experiencing the full weight of grief in my early sobriety.

By then I had earned enough money to buy a well-used

Toyota Tercel. I opened a bank account and even paid for car insurance. When the Tercel died, I leased a brand-new Suzuki Forenza. I was finally approaching my life like a responsible adult, and I did it all on my own. It was the first time I felt proud of myself for something other than cooking.

After a while my parents came to visit me in Miami, but as soon as they got off I-95 my mom started freaking out. "Why would you want to live here?" my mother asked before she had even gotten out of the car. In the past her comments would have angered me, but I stayed calm and reminded myself that she still didn't know the details of everything I had been through. The studio in Little Haiti was a palace compared to some of the other places I'd called home. Slowly I grew to accept my mother for who she is. I was more determined than ever to create my own world.

CHAPTER TWELVE

Bain-Marie

Bain-marie: Also known as a water bath or double boiler, a bain-marie is a container filled with hot water to heat materials gradually to a fixed temperature or to keep them warm over a period of time.

While I was living in Miami and working at City Cellar, my sister Joee moved to New York City. My parents planned a trip for the three of us to fly up and visit her there, and I immediately started bugging them about making reservations at Gordon Ramsay at the London Hotel. I didn't know much about Ramsay's food, but I knew his reputation as a perfectionist chef with an appetite for destruction. What really intrigued me was what I'd heard about his show, *Gordon Behind Bars*, on which he visited an English prison, set up a kitchen called the Bad Boys' Bakery, and taught twelve inmates how to cook. The idea of filming this show in jail made me laugh, and I imagined how a collection of hardened inmates with zero impulse control handled it when Ramsay inevitably starting cursing and yelling at them.

But as the four of us sat down at his restaurant in New York and I eased into a beige chair, jail was the last thing on my mind. I looked around, taking it all in. The lighting at

Gordon Ramsay was soft and low, all from candles instead of lamps. The silverware was first-rate Christofle; I had never held a fish knife that was so small and flat. The hand-crafted Bernardaud china, with its unique patterns, was the perfect balance of contemporary and traditional. Instead of gilded walls or fresco-covered ceilings, like at Alain Ducasse's Le Louis XV in Monte Carlo, there were mirrors everywhere that gave the place a cool, elegant vibe.

I eagerly grabbed the menu and began to study it.

Roasted Foie Gras with green apples, turnips, watercress, and smoked duck

Ravioli of lobster, langoustine, and salmon poached in a light bisque, oscietra caviar, and sorrel velouté

Bresse pigeon with grilled polenta, smoked ventrèche, braised shallots, and dates

Mango, jasmine, and passion fruit soup

Lemonade parfait with honey, bergamot, and sheep's milk yoghurt sorbet

This was different from anything I'd seen in Florida—a contemporary menu completely built on French ideas and techniques. When our food arrived, I was equally impressed. The appetizer of Roasted Foie Gras was luscious, perfectly cooked, and delicately topped with Maldon, chopped chives, and truffle. The Ravioli of Lobster was flavorful and blended perfectly with the saltiness of the caviar and the pungency of the sorrel velouté. The touch of bergamot added character and gave a distinct flavor to the flawless Lemonade Parfait.

I was even more in awe of the presentation—the precision and craft executed on the plate was extraordinary. I could tell that each herb, garnish, and dribble of sauce had been thoughtfully arranged. Staring at the parfait, I marveled at the geometry of the tulles, which were suspended over a symmetrical arrangement of honey drops. This wasn't just food; this was art. The waitstaff operated like synchronized swimmers, clearing and serving in unison with equal parts strength and endurance. I could feel my blood pressure rising with what I can only describe as a culinary boner. Anthony Bourdain would have called that meal "food porn." I left the table feeling titillated and wanting more, only vaguely aware that this level of excitement was dangerous for someone like me.

Before we left, I asked for the restaurant's manager. "This may sound kind of weird," I told him, "but I'm a chef in Miami, and I'd love to work here."

"Send me an email," he told me distractedly, "and I'll forward it to the chef."

I knew Gordon Ramsay probably received a million fucking résumés a month, most of which never saw the light of day. Still, I wasn't going to miss this opportunity. At the hotel I fired off the most sycophantic email I could conjure. Even I nearly got sick reading about my training and passion for food and how I would move heaven and earth for an opportunity to work at a restaurant the caliber of Gordon Ramsay. But I meant every word.

The next day my parents and I were standing in the American Airlines terminal at LaGuardia Airport waiting for our flight back to Florida. Pearl Jam's *Vitalogy* was cranking on my iPod. When I heard the call to start boarding, I stood up, grabbed my backpack, and headed for the gate. Then my cell phone rang. "Mr. Schenker, it's Dale McKay, the sous chef at Gordon Ramsay. I'd like to set up a stage with you."

"Stage" is a French cooking term meaning "trial," and it basically means that a cook goes to a restaurant and trails the chefs around the kitchen. I could hardly speak. "Dale, you know I have a job in Florida," I told him. "But I can be back here in a week."

"That's not a problem," he told me.

I hung up the phone in shock and forced myself to breathe. Slowly I came back to reality. I heard voices. "Jesse, the flight's about to take off." It was my father. "Let's go!"

The next day I barreled through the door at City Cellar. Jeff was alone in his office reviewing the day's specials. "I need some time off," I said. "I had an offer to stage at Gordon Ramsay in New York."

"Sure, Jesse. You have to do this," Jeff said, offering me his complete support.

I quickly called Dale back and arranged a time to stage, and two days later I flew back to New York and crashed on Joee's couch. I had been told to show up at the restaurant at nine, but I was there at seven. I walked in the back entrance and met Seth, the sous chef at Maze, Ramsay's French-Asian place. He immediately handed me a striped apron and a towel. It was a good fucking thing I had gotten there early.

The chefs had already arrived, wearing their hats, pressed white checks, and Union Jack striped aprons. The men all had short hair and were clean-shaven, and the women wore their hair in neat buns. Each chef had his or her own knife set and tools, which were neatly arranged in a tray. I walked toward a group of chefs who were standing shoulder to shoulder breaking down a fish. They looked like medical students hovering over a cadaver. Surrounding the chefs were brilliant copper-rimmed stoves that glistened like diamonds in the early morning sun.

A French kitchen like Ramsay's runs on a hierarchy, or brigade. There was no line of cooks, and no open flames, like I was used to. Everyone has clear-cut responsibilities in the brigade system, which simplifies the process and eliminates the chaos that happens when everybody flies by the seat of their pants. The chef, or chef de cuisine, is in charge of all kitchen operations—ordering food, supervising each station, and developing menu items. Next up is the sous chef, who answers to the chef, handles scheduling, fills in for the chef, and assists the station cooks. There's the saucier (sauté chef), who deals with sautéed items and sauces. This is seen as a glam position, but it's also demanding as hell. There's a poissonier (fish chef), which sometimes gets combined with the saucier position, and an entremetier (vegetable chef), who handles the hot appetizers and often the soups, vegetables, and starches. In a traditional brigade system like Ramsay's, the garde manger, or larder as they called it, handles the salads and the crudo.

In Florida we had our own stations, but we also ran around like madmen, doing whatever was necessary to get everything done. The brigade system was all new to me, and I stood there taking it all in. I wasn't nervous, though. I had my armor of spirituality and acceptance around me, and I knew everything would work out fine if I did my best and was willing to accept any outcome.

Seth came over with a big, burly guy who looked more like a linebacker than a cook. "This is James," he told me. "You'll be working the meat station together." We shook hands. "Concasse these and then dice them," James said, handing me a five-by-six container of perfectly ripened plum tomatoes. I could feel the adrenaline pumping through my body and forced myself to breathe deep.

Grabbing a pot, I filled it with water and added a dash of salt. One by one, I scored out the back of the tomatoes and cut out the stems. Then I boiled the tomatoes for just a few seconds and spidered them into an ice bath so the skins would peel off easily. I arranged three trays in front of my cutting board—one for the peeled tomatoes, a second for the innards and garbage, and a final tray for the dice. I was hauling ass but trying to focus on working clean. I knew there were no messes allowed in Ramsay's kitchen. We really could have eaten off that floor.

I could feel Seth watching me the whole time, but I used the skills I'd learned in meetings to stay focused in the moment. Finally Seth came over. He was short and bald with massive forearms that made him look like a culinary Popeye. As we talked I was impressed by his passion for and knowledge about food.

My shoulders were already aching when James handed me a case of poussins, the butcher's term for baby chickens. "I want you to poach these in a quart of bouillon with thyme, garlic, bay leaves, and peppercorns," he told me. "You're going to bring the water to two hundred and poach the poussins for eight minutes. Then you're going to shock them, remove the breasts and legs, braise the legs, and roast the breasts."

No fucking problem. I was always fast on my feet, but after a few minutes I could see that this exercise highlighted major flaws in my training. The Ramsay cooks were all Michelin- and International Culinary Center–trained. They had done externships at the world's best restaurants. I lacked their finesse and attention to detail, and this stood out like a sore thumb. Though I had prepared thousands of meals, this degree of precision wasn't part of the culinary DNA in Florida, at least not in the restaurants where I'd worked.

James walked over to me with his arms crossed. At first he didn't say a word, but I could tell he wasn't pleased. "What the fuck are you doing?" he asked me. "You're supposed to preserve the skins!" I looked down at my cutting board. I had cut so deep into the chicken leg that I'd exposed the meat and ruined the skin. "These aren't usable," James said angrily. But how the fuck was I supposed to know? I had no idea that I was supposed to be preserving the skins.

I was golden one minute and shit the next. That's just how it was in Ramsay's kitchen. Gordon Ramsay or Josh would burn through the kitchen out of nowhere and knock a cook down a few pegs for not working clean enough. They took the food very seriously. "Donkey," "dumb fuck," and "fucking idiot" were the most commonly used expressions in that kitchen. The cooks who couldn't take the pressure just bolted, but I wasn't scared. On the streets I had certainly been called worse things than a donkey.

After the poussins, it was time to make tomato jam using the tomatoes I'd concassed earlier. I took the tomatoes, tossed on a little olive oil, and sweated them in a deep sauce pot. A lot of the dishes being made around me were amazing.

The techniques were inspiring. But this fucking tomato jam was the dumbest thing I'd ever seen. Why take all the time to peel and perfectly dice a case of tomatoes just to cook them down into mush?

When it was time for service, I stood next to the pass—the place where we plated the food—and watched the food glistening as the chefs called out orders.

"Two frisée, followed by scallops, followed by bream, followed by short rib."

"Oui, Chef," the cooks cried out in unison.

"It's going on two and a half," the meat cook called.

"It's going on one minute," the fish cook responded.

The meat cook led the team. "Garnish up," he called out. Suddenly, the garnish guy appeared with copper pots and handed them to the sous chef on the pass, who took the garnish out of the pot and arranged it on the plate. "Protein's up," was the cue for the meat guy to lay his fish, chicken, veal, or other protein on a tray covered with perfectly manicured parchment paper. I watched the cooks carefully, memorizing how they switched the hot garnish onto a cool tray so they wouldn't burn the chef's hands.

Next up was crispy skin sea bream, which was passed to the chef to position it precisely on top of the garnish. The chef then finished it off with lemon oil and herbs that he kept in a cool drawer below his waist. "Service!" he yelled at the top of his lungs, and four guys in perfectly tailored suits rushed over, picked up the stainless steel trays that were piled with this exquisitely prepared food, and ran it out to the tables. It was like a military operation, and I loved watching it. I hadn't been prepared for this level of intensity or finesse, but I wanted to learn it all.

By 10:00 P.M. I had logged a fifteen-hour shift. Seth told me to go home. "I'll call you tomorrow," he said.

"No," I told him. "I want to stay." I knew I only had one chance to make a good impression, so I stayed there through the end of service, cleaning the pots and dirty trays until lights out. I picked up discarded towels, swept the floor, helped scrub down the stove, and then stood on top of the hood to clean every inch of it by hand. At 1:00 A.M. I made my way to Joee's apartment and crashed, feeling satisfied and inspired by my day's work.

Seth called me first thing in the morning. "I need you to come in" was all he said. An hour later I was sitting in the same dining room where I had eaten that memorable meal with my family just a few weeks before. But this time I didn't know what I was doing there. A brown woven basket filled with every possible variety of bread was positioned next to my plate. A martini glass came out filled with a tomato consommé jelly, diced bacon brunoise, bacon cream, and a lettuce volute (perfectly puréed green lettuce). I closed my eyes and took a bite. It tasted like the world's best BLT. Wild mushroom risotto with big chunks of lobster and Mascarpone cheese followed on the heels of a rectangular-cut smoked trout with beet batons and crisped fennel chips. They just kept coming, one exhilarating dish after the next. As I was gorging myself I wondered if this was how they were thanking me for my work the day before or if I was being softened up for the kill.

After I finished the last bite of dessert, Dale asked me to come back to the kitchen. "You're hired," he told me. "When can you start?"

I returned to Miami and told Jeff that I'd been offered a position at Gordon Ramsay. He didn't waste one second trying to stop me. He was sad to see me go, but he knew it was a once-in-a-lifetime opportunity. Before I left, they threw a big party for me at City Cellar. It seemed that everyone was happy for me. More important, I was happy for me. I felt confident and ready, like my life was finally starting.

Seth made it clear that there were no stars at Gordon Ramsay. Everyone started at the bottom and worked their way up, with no exceptions. At City Cellar I was a boss, the second in command. I ordered the food, hired and fired staff, and delegated work as I saw fit. But at Gordon Ramsay I started at the larder station, picking frisée lettuce. I knew I was in for a transition.

Frisée is a curly, bushy looking lettuce with leaves that shift in color from pale-green to yellow. I had to clean the frisée in an ice bath, making sure to remove every speck of dirt, dry it in a salad spinner, and cut down the core, making sure to remove the green and yellow leaves. Only the white ones in the center were used for the salad. This was my entire job, but I soon moved up to herbs. Chervil resembles parsley, but its leaves are delicate and curly. I needed the top leaves, and they had to be perfectly stemless, without a hint of yellow or a trace of dirt. Finally I moved to pine nuts. I toasted them in a pan, carefully clipping off the tops with a paring knife before cutting them in half. This was a shitty job, even more tedious than the lettuce detail. But I hung in, gradually working my way up through the station.

Two separate dining rooms—Gordon Ramsay (fine dining) and Maze (the more casual dining room)—shared the same kitchen. Competition was encouraged among the chefs, and the atmosphere was often tense. One day a cook was basting fish with butter in a cast-iron pot when the cook standing next to him told him to fuck off. Apparently the butter he was using to baste the fish was burned. The first chef took his basting spoon, which was filled with scalding hot butter, and splashed it on the other cook's arm, leaving him with third-degree burns.

I had been working the larder station for a week before Gordon Ramsay finally came through. He didn't disappoint. Gordon was tall and intimidating, a strong presence to say the least. He walked over to each station and tasted what each of us was making. Then he paused and just stared at each of us with hollow, expressionless eyes.

That night I watched Gordon Ramsay expedite the fine dining pass. He called checks, speaking so quickly that I couldn't understand him. When one dish came out, Gordon was upset because the cook had mistimed the meat. "Fucking donkey," he screamed at him before ordering him off the line. The cook ran down the stairs, crying. Gordon was a perfectionist—I've never met a great chef who wasn't—and demanded only the best. The good cooks were smart and came up with ways to make sure he was always happy. If he asked for a piece of lamb loin, they brought him several. This way he could choose which one he wanted to plate and didn't get angry if one of them was imperfectly cooked.

Part of my job was to clean the walk-in refrigerators. Pulling back every rack, scrubbing them by hand, and washing the floors felt like being back in jail. But I didn't just clean. I made sure everything was labeled, I sorted through the herbs, and then I rolled bunches of chives in wet paper towels to keep them fresh. Even the most menial tasks required my utmost focus and attention to detail. There was no room for error.

One night I was getting pounded. I had five salads, tuna, BLTs, smoked trout, and a million other dishes thrown at me at the same time. The smoked trout had to be timed with the scallops from the hot station, which was tricky because scallops are a food that cannot be overcooked. But I got so backed up that I fucked up. The scallops were ready before I was ready with the trout, and Seth grabbed the tray, bringing it down with the full force of his body, screaming, "Jesse, what the fuck is wrong with you?"

That was it. I'd had enough. I had been working my ass off, and I finally answered back. "Fuck you. You think you fucking intimidate me?"

"Get the fuck out of the kitchen," Seth yelled back.

I grabbed my gear and threw it off the line, stormed downstairs, and packed up my stuff. I was done.

The next day I got a text message from Seth that read, "Let's talk."

I knew I had overreacted, and I took ownership of that. Seth was gracious but stern. "You can't ever do that again," he told me. "I'm your superior. You've got to respect my authority."

I put my head down and got back to work, and after a few

weeks I moved to the fish side, making risotto and working the fryer. I was assigned the cauliflower beignets, little bits of curry-seasoned, deep-fried cauliflower that were part of the scallop dish. The fish cook dusted the scallops lightly with curry powder, sliced them in half, pan-fried them in oil, placed them on a tray, and handed them to the pass. Meanwhile, I cooked the cauliflower beignets and brought them to the pass, where they were placed on top of a silky cauliflower puree. Like everything else in the Ramsay kitchen, it was a well-oiled operation that relied on precise timing. We all dreaded the thought of being late with our food. When that happened, it was time to duck.

"Jesse, what the fuck are you doing?" The unimaginable had happened—my cauliflower beignets were timed imperfectly and the scallops had been left waiting. A temporary head chef on the fine dining side picked up my tray of beignets and hurled it right at me. The tray smacked me hard in the chest before spilling to the floor. Part of me wanted to haul off on him, but I knew that would have been it for me, so I took a breath and got it together. My heart was still beating a mile a minute as I grabbed a broom and a dustpan. I was demoralized but also determined. I just pushed on.

After I'd crashed for a few months on Joee's couch, she'd had enough of me. I rented a cramped studio apartment above a McDonald's in East Harlem, which was still a somewhat rough neighborhood with groups of guys hanging out on every corner. I found places in Harlem to attend meetings, but I didn't have a local meeting that I attended regularly. Still, I made sure that I adhered to all of the principles of recovery by buying food for the homeless guys on my block and getting to work early to set up the other cooks' stations. This was how I stayed sober.

In recovery I had been happy to hand the reins of my life over to a higher power, but the excitement I felt from the food at Gordon Ramsay sparked something in me. Little by little, I took my will back and started making my own plans for the future. Walking around the West Village one day, I called my father and told him, "This is where we have to be." I started thinking about opening my own restaurant, and before long it was all I could think about. My ambition started bubbling over, gradually pulling me to the extremes I'd worked so hard to avoid.

In the meantime I wanted to learn everything I could from Ramsay's kitchen, so I worked as much as possible. On my days off, Seth often called to ask if I wanted to pick up an extra shift. He knew I'd be game. If I was scheduled to work lunch, I stayed through dinner. I worked seven doubles in a week without batting an eye. Some weeks I walked out with a $2,000 paycheck. I could see Seth holding back. He didn't want to hand me a check that was bigger than his, but I earned it. I was so consumed with work that after a couple of months I started going to meetings once a week instead of twice a week. Still, I kept my armor of recovery close around me.

Finally I made it to the meat side of the kitchen. My favorite dish was Beef Tongue 'n' Cheek. I braised beef cheek with a mixture of chopped celery, onions, and carrots, and then I let the cheek cool before shredding it and adding sherry vinegar and parsley. I flattened the cheek in a Cryovac bag, then took cured veal tongue, sliced it thin, and laid it on plastic wrap. I placed the beef cheek in the middle and rolled it into a cylinder so it resembled a pinwheel of tongue wrapped with cheek. Then I sliced it into round pucks, put a little flour on one side, and pan-fried the whole thing. We served it with a generous piece of veal loin, sweet potato purée, and fried spaetzle with crispy veal sweetbreads. It was the most delicious thing I'd tasted at Gordon Ramsay.

Since Ramsay had an empire in the U.K., there were always new chefs coming through the restaurant. One of those chefs, Ian, was working the pass one day. He was screaming at me, calling for times. "Three minutes," I yelled back, but three minutes later the fish was ready and I still didn't have the sweetbreads crispy enough. He threw the sizzle tray with the sweetbreads on it right at me. Again, they hit me in the chest and spilled everywhere. Another cook named Ed, who's now my sous chef, was working at the fish station. He saw in my eyes how pissed off I was. As I rushed right at Ian, Ed quickly moved in front of me, grabbed my arm, and pushed me back to my station. "Chill the fuck out," he told me. "Do you want to get fired?"

Ian was always on my back about something. I don't know if he didn't like me or if he was just out to prove a point, but I became his personal whipping boy. I respected Ian. He was a great fucking cook, and I learned a lot from him, but the competition at Ramsay got the best of us.

On New Year's Eve I was working alongside a guy named Lanning. He was cooking the meat as I worked the garnish. I stepped away to grab some herbs when I heard Ian yelling, "Get rid of all this!" He made Lanning throw out his entire mise en place—everything he needed to cook with—right in the middle of service. That kind of shit happened all the time.

I knew I'd have to walk a fine line as long as I was work-ing for someone else. I had learned what I needed from Ramsay—the precision, organization, and finesse—and I knew I'd make good use of this experience in another kitch-en. It was time for me to start making other plans. But this time I wouldn't settle for some other chef's kitchen. There was a fire inside of me, I was back in the driver's seat, and it was time to act. I wanted more, and this was my chance to grab it—all or nothing.

CHAPTER THIRTEEN

Marinate

Marinate: To immerse foods in an acidic liquid to tenderize and flavor them.

The Savoy Bakery sat at 110th Street and Third Avenue, right in the heart of East Harlem. Only a half-block from my apartment, Savoy stood out like a sore thumb amid the filthy Chinese takeouts, Dominos, dollar stores, and a run-down branch of the New York Public Library. Most mornings I lined up outside the door with a dozen or so other people who stopped at the bakery to grab a cup of coffee on their way to work. Savoy's exposed-brick interior was neat and clean, and the service was quick and courteous. Brian Ghaw, the owner, had an easygoing manner that suggested he always had time to talk.

One day as Brian handed me my coffee his eyes stopped at the tattoo on my left forearm: it's a Japanese slicer, my favorite knife to cook with.

"Where do you work?" he asked me.

"Gordon Ramsay at the London."

Brian told me it was one of his favorite restaurants. Soon we started shooting the shit every morning when I got my coffee and eventually began spending time together, going out to dinner, and trading kitchen stories. Brian introduced me to Christina Lee, who was working in the pastry department at Per Se, one of New York's best restaurants. The three of us started hanging out together and having fun sharing our passion for and experiences with food.

One night when we were out at dinner Christina and I started talking about how much fun it would be to cook together. We seemed to share a lot of the same ideas about food and were definitely both sick of the daily grind of working for someone else, busting our asses to execute another chef's vision instead of our own. Neither of us had the experience or capital to open a restaurant, but we wanted to do something on the side to have fun and earn a little extra income.

I didn't really care about the money. My expenses were low, and I was doing fine working at Gordon Ramsay. But I was motivated by my constant need to create and wanted to find a better outlet for my extra energy than spending my week working doubles in another chef's kitchen.

On my rare days off from Ramsay, I started staging at other restaurants, always looking to learn something new. This is something a lot of chefs do to gain experience in different kitchens. Sometimes I staged where Christina worked at Per Se, a three-star, Michelin-rated restaurant across the street from Central Park. The kitchen was under the command of Jonathan Benno, a chef renowned for his craft and no-nonsense approach to food preparation. Like Ramsay, Per Se was equal parts culinary artistry and first-rate service.

Per Se's signature appetizer was Oysters and Pearls, a dish

created by Thomas Keller at French Laundry. It was a sabayon (a French version of the Italian dessert zabaglione, which is made with egg yolks, sugar, and a sweet wine) of pearl tapioca, Island Creek oysters, and a spoonful of sturgeon caviar plated in a porcelain bowl. Next out of the kitchen was a torchon of duck foie gras served with a crystallized apple chip, some celery-branch batons, Granny Smith apple marmalade, candied walnuts, frisée, and juniper-balsamic vinegar. I looked into the dining room and saw the hungry diners spreading it on perfectly crisped pieces of brioche toast that the waitstaff replaced every minute like clockwork.

It went on like this for hours: course after course just kept coming out. I realized that the little plates of food were timed to keep the diners satisfied but also hungry for more. Per Se wasn't a place to go looking for a quick bite. These diners spent hundreds of dollars on one meal and stretched the experience over four or five hours. Sometimes they even took a tour of the kitchen before leaving. I could see that a meal at Per Se wasn't only about the food. It was an experience, a total immersion of the senses.

Other days I staged at Jean Georges, where I worked the grill. Just like at Ramsay, I studied, watched, and listened. One day Jean Georges walked in wearing his pristine white jacket, long white apron, and Prada shoes. He shook my hand, and as he moved on to greet the other cooks I couldn't stop staring at him, thinking, *He's got what I want.* Jean Georges owned the kitchen, commanded the room, and demanded his staff's respect. The food was different than at Ramsay or Per Se. It was simpler and cleaner. They used Asian ingredients I had never seen in a fine dining restaurant. One of the best dishes I tasted there was Trout Tartar with Horseradish Yuzu Draped in Trout Roe.

Once we started talking about it, Christina and I couldn't get the idea of a side business out of our minds. We scoped out the competition and started taking turns cooking for each other at Savoy, getting a sense of how our separate visions could work together. The great thing about Savoy was that it was only open until 5:00 P.M., and then it sat empty all night long. I already had one foot out the door at Gordon Ramsay, and I felt emboldened by my experiences at Per Se and Jean Georges. Working for another chef, even a great chef, wasn't enough for me. I wanted to strike out on my own and become an entrepreneur.

Before I did anything, I sought my dad's advice. I had always looked up to him as a smart businessman, and I told my dad about what I'd learned at Ramsay, Per Se, and Jean Georges, laying out my idea for him. Right away he recognized my entrepreneurial spirit and nurtured it, reminding me not to get too excited and to carefully review the downside of starting my own business. "You remind me of myself," he told me before adding, "I think you should go for it."

This was the vote of confidence I needed to approach Brian and Christina with an idea to open an after-hours supper club at Savoy. They said yes right away, and we each chipped in $1,000 to turn this dream into a reality. We dove in headfirst, forming an LLC, creating a website, and going to Costco, Restaurant Depot, and IKEA to pick out linens, glassware, flatware, and dishes. Once we had our equipment, we needed a name. My friend Andre from Parkland was living in New York, and one night we went out to dinner and I described my plans for a supper club with French-influenced food and techniques. Andre had spent a lot of time in France, and I told him that I needed one word that perfectly summed up my vision. He didn't hesitate. "Recette," he said immediately. "It means 'recipe.' "

Two weeks later Recette Private Dining held its first event, a ten-course tasting for eight people. After Savoy closed shop for the day, Brian, Christina, and I swooped in and transformed the place from a bakery into a fine dining venue with candles and flowers on the tables and even a sommelier we hired to help select wines. Among the ten courses we served were Hamachi Toro with Porcini Gelée and Baby Artichoke Tortellini with Diver Scallops and Sweet Peas.

One of the diners that night worked at *Daily Candy*, and the next day she wrote a rave review of our meal, comparing it to a great kiss that had passion, skill, and intrigue. That was all it took for the floodgates to open. We all still had other jobs and had planned on doing only one event per week, but already emails and calls were pouring in with many more requests than we could possibly accommodate.

The staff at Ramsay caught wind of my extracurricular activities and started giving me shit. I tried not to let it faze me, but I could feel myself being pulled in too many directions and my anxiety level starting to rise. Then Josh called me into his office. "Do you work for Recette?" he asked me. "I need to know if you work for them or me."

"There is no 'them,' " I told him. "I work for me."

I gave my notice the next day. It felt surreal to walk away from the job I had once wanted more than anything in the world, but I couldn't let that same job slow me down now.

Of course my last two weeks at Ramsay were a living hell. The staff made sure I knew where I stood, and Josh even relegated me to making family meals in the basement canteen instead of cooking for the restaurant's diners. I didn't care. If my years on the streets and in recovery had taught me anything, it was not to sweat the small stuff. Down in the canteen I made the best fucking family meals those guys had ever eaten. I wasn't going to let their resentment dampen my fire.

It was right around this time that I got an email from Lindsay, whom I'd first met back in eighth grade. There was always something special about her—her sparkling green eyes, porcelain skin, and sweet, soothing voice. Lindsay had shown up at a few of my house parties back in the day, and we had even hooked up a couple of times in high school, but she was an honors student with strict parents and never could have kept up with my partying back then. It's a good thing too. She was smart and popular, and had a lot going for her. If we'd gotten together back then, I probably would have ruined everything.

But Lindsay never completely left the picture. While attending the University of Florida, she stayed in touch with Andre and Charnam, who sometimes told me that she asked about me. Then drugs got my undivided attention, but when I heard from her this time things were completely different. Her email simply stated that Andre had sent her the link to Recette Private Dining, and she was happy to see that I was doing what I loved. I was so excited to hear from her that I immediately wrote a long response apologizing for all the ways I'd possibly mistreated her in the past and telling her how beautiful I thought she was.

Over the course of just a few subsequent emails I could tell that Lindsay totally got me. She not only respected everything I had gone through and overcome, but understood it on a very deep level. Lindsay's problems were very different from mine, but her life hadn't been easy either, and we clearly spoke the same language of struggle and survival.

Even though Lindsay was living in California and our first conversations were by phone, they were incredibly intimate as we shared our journeys and travels, holding nothing back. I wanted her, and it made me feel giddy with excitement. Despite the fact that we were living on opposite sides of the country, we have been together ever since that first phone call. Lindsay flew to New York to see me just a few weeks later and then continued to do so every two weeks until she finally packed up her things and moved in with me only six months after sending that first email.

By that time, Recette Private Dining was in full swing. Because The Savoy Bakery was a fully operational business, it took a lot of time to set up for private parties once it closed at the end of the day. It was like creating an entire restaurant from scratch each day and then breaking it down afterward. I didn't mind. This was my focus now, and I threw myself into work more fully than I ever had before. I'd gotten my first taste of success, and I was already hooked.

Every day after the bakery staff left we polished the countertops, emptied the wastebaskets, mopped the floors, and cleaned the toilet. Then we put up the long white table we kept in the bakery's dry storage room. Out came the white linens, which Brian, Christina, and I took turns washing and ironing in between events. We covered the windows with curtains to create privacy. Christina and I prepared the plates, glassware, and silverware, making sure everything was polished. Then it was finally time to prepare the food.

Savoy had big stack ovens for baking bread and convection ovens that were connected to a proofer. Between the ovens were two burners that sat one in front of the other, with a single flame underneath each. Christina turned the convection oven into a French top to keep the pots warm. The back burner always had a pot of boiling water on it for the pasta course, so we were left with one burner to cook with. The stainless steel table turned into our pass. While I cooked, Christina would lay out the plates. I'd pass the puree to her and then come behind her with the garnishes. Or I'd hand a fish tray to her and she'd plate the fish as I came behind her with a sauce. Then we'd add beautiful micro-herbs to enhance the presentation.

Following Thomas Keller's French Laundry model, we just kept the food coming, small, rich plates that we timed out like a ballet. Our goal was for diners to take two or three bites of something and think it was the most delicious thing they'd ever tasted. Then, every time we took a plate away, we had another one ready to go.

This was our show, and we let our creativity run wild. We made gougères, baked pastries that are traditionally filled with cheese, and stuffed them with foie gras mousse. We made Swiss meringue with the consistency of marshmallow creme, folded in pureed foie gras, smeared it across the plate, and then torched it to caramelize it. Then we served it with a perfectly cooked piece of pressed duck breast, Bing cherries, mustard seeds, and a reduction of sherry vinaigrette.

We just kept the plates coming: prosciutto, fresh mozzarella, olives, roasted peppers, cornichons, and grain mustard served with perfectly toasted baguettes; a seafood salad with lightly poached calamari, prawns, fennel, mildly flavored Napa cabbage, and tarragon, dressed with a thinned lemon garlic aioli. Next were roasted forest mushrooms served with thrice-cooked pork belly and goat cheese and lightly seasoned with fresh thyme; peekytoe crab, crispy polenta, and tomato confit mixed with a delicate avocado cream; and asparagus panna cotta and picked fennel laced with grapefruit caviar. We worked tirelessly to make sure that each flavor on the plate was memorable but not so intense that it drowned out the other ingredients.

Soon our calendar was packed with dinner parties, sometimes months in advance. Christina and Brian seemed a little overwhelmed. After all, Brian was still consumed by the bakery, and by then Christina had moved from Per Se to Caffe Falai, an Italian café and pastry shop on the Lower East Side. But Recette Private Dining was my whole world, and I wasn't satisfied with "only" cooking one ten-course dinner party a night.

Lindsay jokes that she should have been on the payroll from the moment she came back into my life, and it's absolutely true. Even though she had a day job at a publishing house, Lindsay worked to make my dreams come true from the very beginning, writing emails, preparing recipe sheets, writing marketing materials, and even serving, busing tables, or playing coat-check girl when needed. She did whatever I asked and seemed happy to do it. She saw that I had a vision and needed someone to lay the bricks, and she laid every single one.

The calls and emails kept pouring in. It was raining, but we didn't have enough buckets to collect all the water. I wasn't going to let that stop me. The same determination that once drove me to score drugs every day and later pushed me through eighty-hour workweeks at Ramsay was now going to put Recette Private Dining on the fucking map. When I wasn't at Savoy, I was scouring Craigslist for people who were looking for a private chef. Soon I was cooking for the owner of one of the city's biggest event production management companies. Through Brian, I met Daniel, who was a wealthy friend of Brian's father's who lived in New Jersey and was looking for a personal chef. Daniel wasn't a gourmet, but he was very specific and knew what he wanted—egg-white frittatas, mushroom soup, baked salmon, chicken potpie, and turkey meatballs, all made to his exact specifications.

As his private chef, I had to prepare all of Daniel's lunches and dinners for the week. Every day, I got to the bakery at 8:00 A.M. and sidestepped the bakery chefs as I cleaned off a fresh chicken, removed the legs and wings, and dried them thoroughly before seasoning them with salt, fresh oregano, and fresh ground pepper. I stuffed the cavity with fresh orange slices, thyme leaves, garlic, and half an onion. Then I put the chicken in the convection oven and roasted it three-quarters of the way through. I didn't want to cook it all the way or it would dry out when Daniel heated it up later. Then

I tossed in some roasted broccoli mixed with fresh herbs and olive oil and wrapped it in foil. If Daniel wanted a sandwich, I prepared fresh sliced turkey with avocado or made chicken salad with poached chicken, apples, and walnuts and mixed it together with lemon and olive oil instead of mayonnaise. I packed all the food in Tupperware containers and loaded it into my rental car for the forty-five-minute drive to Alpine, New Jersey. After driving back to the city, I started prepping for the next party.

This schedule left little time for meetings or even reflection. I hardly had time to sleep. But I was still connected to other addicts, and once in a while one of them would remind me to come to a meeting. Then months would pass before they tracked me down and reminded me to come again. I was on a tear like the one Gibson and I had been on in Orlando, but instead of crack I was bingeing on work.

One wintry night I was driving down Route 9 on my way to Daniel's. The roads were covered in ice, and I felt myself losing control of the rental car as it began to slide and slip. I let go of the wheel and just prayed for the best: the car completely spun around two times before smashing into the guardrail. The back window was covered in chicken potpie, and I had bits of chicken salad in my hair. The entire driver's side door was smashed in, and the front rim and bumper were bent inward so much that the car was nearly impossible to drive.

I tried to keep driving up Route 9 in my wrecked car. I was sore and my shoulder was definitely dislocated, but I was determined to get Daniel what was left of his food. After I'd been trudging along at a tedious pace for a few minutes, a police car pulled up behind me. "Turn off your engine and step out of your car with your hands up," the cop announced through his speaker.

I couldn't open the driver's side door, so I crawled into the passenger's seat and kicked it open with a vengeance. My frustration and anger bubbled up, and I started cursing at the officers at the top of my lungs. "You fucking pigs!" I shouted. "I'm the one who got in an accident, and you're telling me to put my fucking hands up?" The snow was falling harder as the two cops walked over to me with their hands firmly on their holsters.

"Calm down, sir," one of them said. "We got word of an accident, and you continued to drive in these conditions. What are we supposed to think?" I knew exactly what they thought because just a few years prior it would have been true. But I explained to them about Daniel and the food in the back of the car. After running my name, the cops helped me get a tow truck for the rental car. Then I walked the remaining two miles to Daniel's house, in the snow, holding a sheet pan with the remaining food.

The Recette Private Dining requests kept coming in. I said yes to everything. "We'll figure it out," I told Christina and Brian every time I accepted a seemingly impossible event. I just kept upping the ante, taking on more and more. One Monday night I prepared a five-course tasting for twelve at a mansion in Rhinebeck. On Thursday I created an elegant dinner for six at a Philadelphia townhouse. Then I answered a Craigslist ad from a family looking for a weekend chef at their home in the Hamptons. I stayed in a cottage on the grounds and cooked every meal from breakfast Friday morning through Sunday brunch before driving back to the city.

At every one of these events I never stopped working the room, using the same skills I'd used to score drugs, pull off scams, and hustle people out of their money to take Recette Private Dining to another level. If I needed a fresh lamb shank for dinner and none was available, I didn't get mad. I just found a way to manipulate the meat guy into giving me a lamb shank that he'd promised to another customer. If a client was on the fence about hiring us to cater a party for forty, I guided her in the right direction. "It's your decision," I'd tell her. "But I can guarantee the food will be memorable." Just like I had done on the streets of Broward, I put on a show.

Of course, recovery requires rigorous honesty, not only with other people but also with yourself. As I slid down the slippery slope of addiction once again—this time to work instead of drugs—I stopped being honest with myself. Instead of accepting that I was powerless and relinquishing control, I feverishly grabbed the reins and drove myself further and further away from the peace I had finally found.

By then Joee had been in the salon business for years, working her way up the food chain from receptionist to manager at Paul LaBrecque, a high-end salon and spa with a few locations around the city. Joee's boss was into the New York food scene and had heard about Recette Private Dining. One of his locations had a little coffee bar, and he was looking to turn it into a café that served sandwiches, pastries, and coffee for clients and staff. "Do what you want," he told me. "I just want food here."

It was the perfect setup. There wasn't much money involved, but I didn't have to pay rent and I got to keep whatever cash I made. Plus, I could buy my pastries directly from the Savoy at a discount. My schedule got even busier. I got to Savoy at 8:00 A.M. to start prepping for Daniel. At 9:00 I switched over to making sandwiches and selecting pastries for the salon. I left for the salon at 10:00, and from 11:00 A.M. to 3:00 P.M. I stood behind a makeshift bar at Paul La-Brecque selling food. Then I went back to Savoy to finish prepping Daniel's food. By 4:00 P.M. I was in my rental car on the way to New Jersey so I could get back to the bakery by 7:00 to execute a dinner I'd prepped the night before.

Recette Private Dining's events grew bigger and bigger. Soon we were catering weddings, corporate events, Fashion Week tents, and launch parties for Delta, Evian, and other blue-chip companies. Through Joee, I met a guy named Andrew who worked in events and had been hired to coordinate the VH1 Hip Hop Honors. He needed a caterer. "First we need to set up a tasting for VH1 in their production studio," he told me. "You game?"

"Fuck, yeah," I told him without bothering to ask about the details. When I told Brian and Christina about the event, they both thought I'd lost my mind. "It's too much," Christina said. But I just kept pushing.

To get the VH1 gig we had to come up with a hip-hop-themed tasting menu for Andrew and his staff at the production company. We took Southern favorites and put our own spin on them using modern French techniques. The chicken legs were braised in a classic coq au vin style with wine, lardons, and mushrooms, but I added some zing with jalapeños and cumin. Instead of regular meatballs, I selected a mixture of pork cuts that would enhance the flavor. There were also cornbread sliders, watermelon coleslaw, pulled pork sandwiches, and pecan pie bites. The menu went on and on.

Andrew and his staff loved it and hired us on the spot. We'd be cooking for 1,400 people at the Hammerstein Ballroom. Even I knew we were in way over our heads. We had only enough equipment to cook for a dozen or so people at Savoy, and the last time I cooked for this many people had been in jail, where I wasn't even allowed to use salt. I quickly pulled in resources from everywhere I could think of. First I called every cook I respected who might want to earn some extra cash, and then I called friends, relatives, and neighbors who I thought would be willing to help.

The day before the party Brian closed Savoy two hours early. The rental company truck pulled up with all of our equipment, and we filled the entire front of the bakery with stack warmers that each held up to thirty hotel pans. Then we commenced cooking, all of us working through the night to get it all done. The next morning I called my cousin Keith, who was living in New York, and asked for his help. Together we went up to the Bronx and rented a huge U-Haul to transport our food and equipment to the event. Back at Savoy, we got everything into the back of the truck. Brian was driving, and Christina sat in the passenger seat.

The rest of us—me, my cousin Keith, and Ed from Gordon Ramsay—looked at each other, then silently climbed into the back of the truck. We were squeezed in between dozens of boxes, crates, and warmers, and when the door to the U-Haul was shut, we were plunged into total darkness. As Brian drove we lost our bearings and had to reach out to grab onto giant food warmers to steady ourselves. Brian wove in and out of New York City traffic and we were tossed around like rag dolls, bumping into boxes and knocking over stack warmers. When Brian stopped at a light, I momentarily got my bearings and used my cell phone to create some light and call Christina. "Tell Brian to slow the fuck down," I told her, but I knew he needed to haul ass to get to the Hammerstein Ballroom in time.

Suddenly the U-Haul came to a stop, and I heard the engine turn off. Finally! I looked at my phone. It was 1:45. We had the use of the service elevator to load in all of our shit only from 2:00 to 3:00. Then I heard someone yell, "You can't park that thing here!" The back of the truck opened, and sunlight came pouring in. Surrounding us were literally hundreds of people—police, security detail, and producers—and they were all looking right at us. "Move the fucking truck," a cop yelled again.

Everyone looked at me, dumbfounded. We had to get pre-heated food up to the second floor for 700 staff members and then get to the balcony floor to prepare food for all of the performers and their guests. Suddenly my mind cleared. "Get your asses out of the van and let's go!" I opened the rail, dropped the latch, and started pushing all the food and supplies down a ramp positioned at the back of the U-Haul. One by one, we loaded each of the warmers into the elevator. While Keith parked the van, we brought the staff food to the fifth floor. The warmers had to be plugged in, but the power was out. Everyone was freaking out, but I ran from floor to floor until I found an electrician who could fix the problem.

In full delegation mode, I made sure everything was on

point for the staff food and then moved to the VIP room and started setting up the tables. Ed and I set up a station on each side of the stage and started pumping out food. We had brought a walkie-talkie system so I could check in with Christina and Brian in the other areas, but it didn't really work, so I ran up and down the stairs all night, checking on everything, in between cooking for the VIPs.

The next day it was like none of it had ever happened. I was back at Savoy at 8:00 A.M. to cook for Daniel, make sandwiches for the salon, and prep for a private party that night. It was a hustle just like any other, and I loved the intensity. I literally couldn't get enough.

CHAPTER FOURTEEN

Terrine

Terrine: A French forcemeat, or a coarsely chopped mixture of ground, lean meats emulsified with fat and properly combined to create a uniform and sliceable texture.

Somewhere in the midst of all this insanity, my childhood friend Mike Charnam moved into my tiny apartment above McDonald's, which Lindsay also moved into shortly thereafter. After a long day at Savoy, the salon, New Jersey, and back to Savoy for a dinner party, we'd stay up late into the night working on the business plan for my first restaurant. I was full of passion and excitement, but I was determined to use the lessons my dad had taught me over the years and think everything through before making any decisions.

First we did market research. Late at night, after finishing a seemingly endless day of work and then serving a ten-course tasting menu, I took Lindsay to every decent restaurant in Manhattan and ordered half the menu. At the original John Dory in the Meatpacking District I savored the Oyster Pan Roast with Uni Butter. At Craft Bar I fell in love with the Pork Belly Roulade. But most of all I was inspired by Thomas Keller's French Laundry model of small plates of fully composed dishes. At more traditional restaurants I'd order a piece of salmon and get sick of the flavor after just a few bites. I didn't want this to happen to my guests, and I soon had a vision of serving small plates of scrumptious food that people could share, enjoying a wide variety of textures and flavors.

Once I had a clear vision for the food, we priced out everything from plates, spoons, glassware, linens, and wine to office supplies. I spent hours thinking about what type of music we would play and toying around with dozens of color schemes. I knew what mood I wanted to create and who my customers would be. I made up a menu of Mediterranean-influenced dishes incorporating ingredients from the land and sea. I wanted to serve salty, briny, boldly seasoned food, so I made a list of thirty items and costed out the dishes using rough recipes as placeholders. Then I crafted work schedules and profit-and-loss statements, even though I hadn't yet hired one fucking employee.

One night we were up late talking about the food, the music, and the menu, and I could tell that Mike and Lindsay were exhausted. But I was full of energy as I ran around the apartment putting on different music to see what kind of vibe I wanted to create. "You're an animal," Mike screamed at me. Without thinking, I began roaring at him. "I am an animal," I yelled back. The three of us burst out laughing, but what Mike said was true—there was something inhuman about my relentless pursuit.

Before I had any investment money, I walked the city with dozens of brokers to get to know the real estate market—the locations, the foot traffic, and the cost per square foot. By the time I was done I knew exactly what I wanted and what I needed to open a small, forty-seat restaurant in the West Village.

Once we completed the business plan, I knew that I needed to get in front of my father. He'd been a businessman his whole life, and I trusted his opinion more than anyone else's. I knew he couldn't give me all the money I needed, but I thought he would want to get involved. Ever since I'd gotten out of jail, I'd wanted to somehow pay my parents back for everything I'd taken from them and put them through. I had fantasies about making a lot of money and writing them a big check. This was hardly the same thing, but I still wanted to get them involved in realizing my dream.

My father looked at my business plan and said, "I think it's a great idea. You have to speak to Art." Art Bilger was a childhood friend of my dad's who happened to be an extremely successful venture capitalist. After emailing back and forth with his assistant for weeks, Art agreed to meet me for five minutes in the lobby of the Regency Hotel.

The night before the meeting with Art, I was full of adrenaline and excitement. I kept Lindsay up all night going over the business plan and making sure it was airtight. I knew that even five minutes with someone like Art was a rare opportunity, so I did as much due diligence as possible. It was difficult to have such a strong desire for something that I knew was ultimately out of my hands. I clung to my faith and my acceptance, knowing that as long as I gave it my all, I would be happy with the results.

When Art met me in the lobby, I didn't even show him the business plan. Instead, I shared my passion, telling him about the kind of atmosphere and food I wanted to create. "Come up to my room," he said. "Let's keep talking." In his lavish hotel room I opened up the business plan and went over it with him line by line. Instead of nodding in approval, he raked it over the coals, challenging me with a million questions about what the demographics had to do with the location, the liquor versus food revenue and percentages, the profit margins, and the labor costs. Thanks to my hours of obsessive study, I had an answer for every one of his questions.

When we were done, Art looked at me and asked, "Do you read the newspaper? Do you know what's going on in the world?" It was 2008. The global economy was tanking, and there I was asking for a capital investment.

"When you're depressed, what do you do?" I asked him. "You eat and drink. I have no doubt this is the right time and we will succeed."

"I'll invest in your restaurant," Art finally said. "Now that you have some capital, it should be easier to find the rest." He reached out and shook my hand.

I left the hotel and skipped down Park Avenue, pausing only to call Lindsay so we could celebrate the moment together. Then I called my father, and when I heard his excitement, I knew there was no one else in this world who would share my passion and enthusiasm like him. I needed someone to be my business partner, to manage the business side of things while I focused on the creative aspects of the restaurant.

"I want you to be my business partner," I told my dad. "It has to be you." My father was getting ready to retire, not looking to get involved in another business, but he was too much like me to say no. He called me back the next day and said, "There's nothing I would rather do more than be in business with my son." He said he would match Art's investment.

Instead of waiting until I had all the money, I kept "acting as if"—making plans for the restaurant as if it was already a reality. Over the next several months I worked on raising the remaining funds and looking for locations in between my regular work for Daniel, the salon, and Recette Private Dining. I found a place on Carmine Street that seemed like a good possibility, and my dad and I brought in a restaurant consultant who had helped open many places in South Florida. Telling us that many of the terms were outrageous, he basically killed the deal. Nothing came easy, but when I started to feel desperate, I made sure to go to a meeting or reach out to other addicts so that I remained in the center of the circle. This way at least I knew that someone would catch me if I fell.

I didn't always know where to turn, but I kept striving forward. I approached many of my wealthy clients and asked them if they wanted to become a partner in the restaurant, but they all passed. Then I asked several people I knew in Florida—some of them friends or business associates of my father's—but they all passed too. Late at night I wondered how many of those people had said no because they knew about my past, but I tried not to think about that since it was beyond my control.

Finally I had another success. My client Daniel had a good history with restaurant investments, but he didn't want to be a partner. Instead, he gave me, a twenty-seven-year-old kid with a record, an unsecured loan for $100,000. His faith in me was truly humbling. Shortly after, my aunt Stacey and uncle Mark joined with an investment. I was filled with gratitude. After clawing my way back from hell, I found myself in the enviable position of having something to come back to—not only a loving and forgiving family, but people of means who saw my drive and passion and were willing to help me. I knew how lucky I was. Many addicts never enjoy this level of emotional or financial support, and I set short- and long-term goals to give back in meaningful ways.

At that point we were almost all the way to our fund-raising goal. The restaurant consultant introduced me to a new broker who showed me two spaces in the West Village, one on Bleecker and the other on West Twelfth Street. When I walked up to the second location and saw the quiet tree-lined corner and French windows, it reminded me of that bustling restaurant at the end of a quiet street in Florence what felt like a lifetime ago. I fell in love and knew in a moment that this was where Recette would live.

When we signed the lease for 328 West Twelfth Street in September 2009, it felt like a hard-won victory, but we didn't have much time to celebrate. I went down to the restaurant right after signing the lease and walked into the kitchen. The ceiling panels were covered in dry grease, the floor tiles were chipped, the sinks were clogged, and the kitchen equipment looked like it was from the turn of the nineteenth century. The kitchen exhaust system consisted of a single fan that would barely have been adequate for a small home kitchen. Otherwise, there was no ventilation. We had to tear it all down and start fresh with a complete kitchen renovation.

We quickly set our sights on a January opening, which gave us only four months to prepare. I hardly knew where to begin. Christina, Brian, and I dissolved Recette Private Dining so I could focus entirely on the new Recette. Every day I got up with the sun and was at the restaurant by 7:00 to meet with architects, liquor lawyers, contractors, electricians, and handymen. There were permits, community boards, and labor unions to worry about in addition to all the little details regarding the restaurant itself.

While I was accustomed to delegating in the kitchen, when it came to the restaurant, I wanted to be involved in every detail. I couldn't let go. My father was meant to handle the business end of things, but I made sure he ran everything by me, even the things I knew nothing about, like leases, insurance binders, attorneys, and landlords. Lindsay was now working at an email marketing company by day, but she came home every evening and jumped right in, typing out emails that I dictated while scrubbing and later measuring every inch of the kitchen on my hands and knees.

I didn't hire a designer. Instead, I told the contractors exactly what I wanted and asked my mother to help with the decor. Then I went down to Crate and Barrel and Pearl River Mart myself to pick out linens, glassware, china, and flatware. On my birthday in October I went to a restaurant supply store on the Bowery and picked out all of our kitchen tools—sheet pans, spatulas, pots, pans, skimmers, tongs, ladles, wooden spoons, basting spoons, and baking supplies. It was the best birthday present I could have imagined.

But I knew the most important thing was to get the kitchen in order. Christina had been an amazing partner in Recette Private Dining, and I wanted her to be my pastry chef. She said yes right away and even became an investor by contributing her own funds. Then I picked two of the guys I most respected from Gordon Ramsay who hadn't given me shit for leaving—Dean and Ed. They were both awesome cooks, fast and efficient and expertly trained by Ramsay to reach the level of execution that I wanted to achieve.

Christina, Ed, Dean, and I spent hundreds of hours in the kitchen creating new recipes for Recette's menu and then tweaking them until they were absolutely perfect. I didn't want to use any of the recipes from Recette Private Dining— everything had to be brand-new. I thought about the dishes I most loved at Hearth and Gramercy Tavern, which had all been perfectly seasoned, in-your-face food. That's what I wanted to serve. We started experimenting. Christina and I made a traditional caramel, but instead of butter, I added sherry vinegar and savory spices, creating a sweet, salty, and acidic sauce that we served with pork belly. I was inspired by Spanish and Portuguese cooking and the way they use meat and seafood together, and after experimenting with different ingredients, I found that rock shrimp paired nicely with the pork belly. This became one of Recette's signature dishes.

There were no rules or boundaries—Asian, Mediterranean, and traditional American ingredients were all fair game. I had the idea for a duck carpaccio that involved curing a duck breast for twenty-four hours and rendering the skin so that it was crispy on the outside but still rare and succulent on the inside. Slicing the duck breast paper-thin, I laid it out like a fan and topped it with chicken liver mousse.

Then I rolled it up and served it with crispy duck tongue. It felt good to be creating something that was completely my own, and during those hours in the kitchen all of the stress and anxiety about opening the restaurant melted away.

Deciding which recipes made it onto the menu wasn't arbitrary. Any chef worth his salt can come up with creative dishes, but it's another thing to come up with ones that can be executed in three minutes by any cook in the kitchen. The final menu items had to be foolproof. At first our ravioli dish consisted of cheese ravioli in a seafood broth with cured pork jowl, cuttlefish, and roasted mushrooms. The broth for the ravioli was delicious—salty and briny and tasting like the ocean—but we noticed that the cheese inside the ravioli sometimes leaked out and curdled in the broth. The dish wasn't ready yet. After weeks of experimenting, we transformed the broth into a shellfish sauce and added cream to make it more viscous. Then we added roasted cauliflower to the ravioli filling so that it held together better. Soon this became one of my favorite dishes.

Instead of fried shrimp or calamari, I wanted to serve fried razor clams. We ordered 150 pounds of razor clams, cleaned them, and dredged them in seasoned flour, egg, and breadcrumbs. Then we fried them and served them with a spicy tomato sauce. I loved this dish, but it was too hard to clean the razor clams, because they were so full of sand, and there was too much room for error when frying them. They came out either overcooked or undercooked too often. To make it to the menu they had to come out perfect at least eight out of ten times.

In many ways my time on the streets and in jail prepared

me well for the crazy process of opening a restaurant in New York City. I had developed a sixth sense about people, and when I needed someone to break down boxes and haul out trash, I had no qualms about walking up to a guy on the street and saying, "Hey, man, are you looking for work? Come with me." When the hot water went out one day and everyone else was paralyzed with panic, I just went outside and circled the block until I found a guy getting into a contractor's van. "Hey, man, I need your help," I said, and he came into the restaurant, cleaned out some insulation and other junk from underneath the pilot light, and relit it within five minutes.

Nothing really fazed me. I wasn't spending time praying or studying the Bible like I had in jail, but I still very much believed in God's will and that everything would happen as it should. The Big Book, which serves as the basis for AA, tells us that acceptance is the answer. Throughout this process I lived by the motto, "Your serenity is in direct proportion to your acceptance." I read this and repeated it to myself every day like a mantra, knowing that being committed to one particular outcome for Recette would mean losing my grip on serenity.

Before our official opening, we did three nights of service for friends and family. This gave us a chance to work out the inevitable kinks in the menu and service, and sure enough, there were plenty of things that needed to be ironed out. The first thing we noticed was that the general manager we'd hired hadn't laid out the tables very well. There was no room between the tables for the servers to walk through and deliver dishes or clear plates. The servers also needed to up their game. Some guests got doubles of the same appetizer; another diner received his dessert before his main course.

The kitchen was under control from day one because I had such a tight team. But there were still some menu items that needed fine-tuning. Some of the charcuterie got cut, and we decided to offer cheese by the piece instead of a cheese plate so the guests could customize their meals. We had a chickpea dish with yogurt, tarragon, and pork belly that we cut from the menu before the official opening because it just wasn't refined enough. I tasted everything that came out of the kitchen; I didn't want the guests to get anything that wasn't absolutely perfect.

By the third night things were running pretty smoothly. I walked outside and looked into the restaurant through the French windows, watching everyone eating and drinking and laughing. The room was filled with joy. *Holy shit*, I thought. *I really created something.* Seven years earlier I'd been living in the mulch in a park, looking forward to nothing in life except my next high. But this new high of knowing I had created something was just as exciting—and just as addictive.

On opening night Recette did sixty covers, the next night we did eighty, and the night after we did a hundred. Within a week we were packing people in. For the most part people seemed to love the food, but others thought the plates were too small and too expensive. I wanted the guests to be happy, so I listened to these criticisms, increasing the portion sizes for some items and lowering the prices on others.

I was surprised that it took just as much work to keep the

restaurant going after the opening as it had to get it open. It was a living organism that needed to be nourished, and I took this on completely like a new mother who won't let anyone else hold her baby. I carried lemon and sea salt with me at all times and reseasoned everything that came out of the kitchen. I didn't trust anyone else to season it as perfectly as I could, and I held the employees to high, sometimes impossible standards. In that first month I definitely yelled more than I should have, but I had a vision that wouldn't be denied. I had to inspect every little plate of food and make sure the servers were on their toes and the hostess wasn't screwing up the reservations.

Some of the people around me thought I was crazy, but the intensity I brought to Recette was no different than the intensity I exhibited as an addict hustling, stealing, and manipulating to get money to buy drugs. For better or worse, I saw every element of the restaurant as a reflection of me. I had taken all the experiences I ever had in a kitchen—from cooking with Rosie and Nana Mae to working my way up the South Florida restaurant food chain, mashing potatoes in jail, working at Gordon Ramsay, and staging at Per Se and Jean Georges—and amalgamated them into my own unique style. I was proud of it, and I couldn't loosen the reins and risk losing everything I had accomplished.

I never sat back and reveled in the moment. Instead, I blindly pushed forward, already thinking obsessively about my next restaurant. I had a vision for a completely different restaurant than Recette, a bigger and more approachable place that people could visit every day. I continued to cater outside events, but Recette didn't have a private dining room, so we had to turn down many requests for private parties. We had only six seats at the bar where people could wait until their table was ready. It was a learning process, and I already saw a second restaurant as a way of removing the restraints we operated under at Recette.

This was when my armor of serenity and connection started to wear away. I continued to say yes to every catering request I possibly could, worked long hours at the restaurant, and then went home to crunch numbers and work on a business plan for a second restaurant. When I wasn't at Recette, I was doing "market research," my term for all-night eating binges on Beef Marrow with Oxtail Marmalade at Blue Ribbon or burgers at Daddy-O. Some nights I went to four restaurants in a row. There were no vacation days or time off. I stopped going to meetings and eventually lost touch with the other addicts I was connected to. In the back of my head was that mantra, "Your serenity is in direct proportion to your acceptance," but as I obsessively tried to control the direction of my career my acceptance slipped away—and my serenity went right along with it.

CHAPTER FIFTEEN

Barding

Barding: To cook meat by wrapping it in a layer of fat, such as pork fatback or bacon, before cooking it.

Three months after Recette opened, Frank Bruni, who had just retired as chief restaurant critic for the *New York Times,* came in with a friend. I noticed him right away. He sat down at table 17, right next to the kitchen, and ordered Salt Cod Fritters, Buffalo Sweetbreads, Sea Trout, and Berkshire Pork Belly with Rock Shrimp. I stayed in the kitchen and made sure to cook everything myself, my hands trembling as I poured the sherry into the caramel sauce for the pork belly. Then I stood at the edge of the kitchen and tried to eavesdrop. Bruni finished everything, which I took as a good sign, but he didn't comment on the food. As soon as he left I exhaled, a huge smile spreading across my face. Whether or not the *Times* reviewed Recette, the very fact that someone like Frank Bruni had gotten wind of it meant we were onto something.

A week later Sam Sifton, who at the time was the chief restaurant critic at the *New York Times,* came into the restaurant. He sat at a table next to the French window with his body facing outward and his face in full view of the security camera and ordered the Wild Arugula with Kumquats, Mint, Lemon, Hazelnuts, and Ricotta Salada and the Poussin with Grits. I tried to cook everything myself, running back and forth behind the line and to the pass to plate the food. Ed hated it when I reached over him and seasoned his fish. I was driving everyone nuts by being so controlling. "Refill his water glass," I shouted to the servers. "Bring more bread to the table!" Once Sifton's food was served, I scrambled downstairs to my basement office and shut the door. For the next hour I kept my eyes glued to the security camera as Sifton ate, studying his facial expressions and trying to pick up on any clue as to whether or not he was enjoying his meal.

I didn't sleep at all that night. Neither did Lindsay, thanks to me. I kept waking her up to ask what she thought. "I don't know, Jesse," she said. "It's late. Go back to sleep." But there was no way I could do that. I was so on edge. So far all of our reviews had been lukewarm and business was starting to level out; we were nowhere near where I wanted or expected it to be. I knew that a review from the *Times* would either make or break us overnight. Even in a world with Menu Pages, Yelp, Zagat's, and a million other places for online reviews, people still pay attention to reviews by people who are paid to write and talk about food. We needed a good review from the *Times*. I wouldn't accept anything else.

A week after Sifton's visit I noticed a reservation under the name "Steve Bedot." I don't know why, but the name jumped out at me. I ran downstairs to the office and asked Lindsay to look into it. A few minutes later Lindsay came running up the stairs so fast that she tripped and fell flat on her face. "The phone number matches the name Sam Sifton used last time," she said. "Sifton's coming back." That's when we knew for sure that a review was pending.

The whole staff was nervous that night when Sam Sifton walked in with three guests. With his head down, not making eye contact with anyone, he made his way to a table in the center of the restaurant. He and his guests ordered half the menu: Salt Cod Fritters with Lamb Sausage Ragu, Spot Prawn Crudo, Chorizo with White Beans, Buffalo Sweetbreads with Pickled Celery and Blue Cheese, Arctic Char with Ocean Broth, Blue Foot Mushrooms, and Pork Belly with Romesco and Rock Shrimp. I told all the servers to spy on him, and as I cooked I kept peeking out from the kitchen. He stayed until closing time, laughing and drinking right through. Clearly, he didn't hate the meal, but I needed more than that.

Two weeks later Lindsay was looking through the reservations when she found another name with a phone number that matched the one used by "Steve Bedot." This had to be a good omen, I told myself. Sifton brought a new group of people and ordered everything on the menu. This time I could tell he was enjoying himself as he ate, drank, laughed, and joked around with his friends and even the waitstaff. He was the last person to leave, and as he was walking out he paused and we locked eyes. Sifton nodded, saying, "Thank you."

A fact checker from the *New York Times* called the following day and fired off a million questions. "How do you make the romesco sauce?" he asked. "Can you list all the ingredients? What about the pork belly? How is it influenced?"

I answered everything, and then he said, "We'll send a photographer," before abruptly hanging up. The next day I carefully laid out cod fritters and pork belly as the photographer snapped away.

It was a slow Tuesday night, and the restaurant was half empty. We were an hour into service when my publicist called. "Are you sitting down?" she asked. I didn't like the mystery and told her to just come out with it. "The *New York Times* is giving you two stars," she said. "And it's written like a three-star review."

I hung up the phone and bolted down the stairs to my office to read the review, which had just been posted online. The entire kitchen staff, along with the majority of our diners, followed. I sat down at my computer with a dozen bodies hovering over me as I scoured the website, looking for the review. Finally the webpage loaded. It was everything Chris had said, but it felt a million times better to read it with my own eyes. Sam Sifton described Recette in exactly the way I'd first envisioned it: "The menu is remarkably free of stuff that's available everywhere else," and, "It hits the flavor stations hard: salty and sweet, with an acidic bite at the end." He understood what I was aiming for and articulated it perfectly, referring to the Foie Gras Terrine as "a meat painting, an organ sculpture," calling the Salt Cod Fritters with Lamb Sausage Ragu "a head-scratchingly good combination," and describing the Pork Belly and Rock Shrimp in Sherry Caramel as "Spain on a plate, as seen from Manhattan."

I looked around the crowded office for Lindsay, and when I found her standing in the corner we hugged, knowing we had done it. Sam Sifton changed my life. From that moment on, Recette was booked every night.

I thought I was busy before, but once I was reviewed in the *New York Times,* everyone wanted a piece of me. Requests for private parties and events poured in, and I continued to say yes to everything from small dinner parties at people's homes to huge catering events at the Cartier mansion. When charities asked for help, I always made a point to say yes and be of service, and I enjoyed cooking for 800 people at City Harvest and Autism Speaks events. Every month I was on a new morning show, each one taking hours of preparation. And then I was back at Recette, trying to get the servers and hostess excited about great hospitality, maximizing the grid so every table was full and turning over efficiently, and scrutinizing the monthly P&Ls. In between, I stuffed myself full of hoagies, French fries, and cheesesteaks, only half aware that my weight was steadily creeping upward. I felt an insane amount of pressure to keep myself out there and relevant. My brain was constantly going, and I began to wake up every morning in a panic, thinking, *What else can I do to move forward?*

Lindsay and I had only been together for about a year and a half, but it already felt like we'd shared a million lifetimes. I knew how lucky I was to have found someone who was so completely supportive of me and my dreams. She had already quit her day job to work at Recette full-time as our operations manager. It certainly felt like Recette was as much hers as it was mine, and I wanted to share the rest of my life with her too. Lindsay and I had never really talked about getting married, but I figured that if she'd already put up with me for this long, she must have been in it for the long haul.

I bought her a ring and planned to surprise her with it over dinner at Scarpetta, a modern Italian restaurant just a stone's throw from Recette. But that night Recette was slammed, and I didn't want to leave. Lindsay was in the office going over the books as I supervised the kitchen. It took everything I had to tear myself away from the restaurant, but I finally did, and over a delicious meal of Polenta with Morels and Truffles, Chilled Pea Soup with Crabmeat and Currants, Mozzarella in Carozza, and Black Cod with Slow-Roasted Tomatoes and Caramelized Fennel, I handed Lindsay the ring, and immediately fumbled. "Look, we don't have to do this now," I said, "but do you accept?" Lindsay still teases me for my unromantic proposal, and I absolutely deserve it.

"Of course I'll marry you," she said, and as we hugged and kissed the other diners all started clapping. True to form, we went right back to work after dinner.

The excitement we felt after getting engaged didn't last long. Only a couple of weeks later my mother felt a lump in her breast and went to get it checked. It turned out that she had an aggressive form of breast cancer, at stage two. I was devastated and worried, but this wasn't my mom's first health scare. Back when I was on the streets, she'd started seeing dots in her vision and got a CAT scan that showed a benign tumor on her brain, right underneath her skull. The doctors watched it for years and had finally decided it had to come out. That was just a few months before Recette had opened. My mom is a warrior, and she approached the brain surgery and now the breast cancer with complete strength and bravery. She never complained through many uncomfortable surgeries, chemo, and radiation. Every time I asked how she was doing she insisted that she was fine.

Lindsay and I toyed around with the idea of a traditional wedding with family and friends, but I knew we'd never take the time off from work to plan a proper wedding. A big circus wedding wasn't really our speed, anyway. Plus, I saw no reason to wait. I wanted a marriage, not a wedding. Lindsay and I got married at the City Clerk's Office on May 28, 2010, at noon and were back to work at four. That night Lindsay hosted at Recette wearing her wedding dress.

Only six days later Lindsay asked me to meet her out in back of Recette. The restaurant was packed, and I didn't want to leave for even a minute, but Lindsay insisted. When I got outside, she was standing there, smiling nervously. I knew what was coming. "Are you pregnant?" I asked her.

"How'd you know?" she asked as I bent down to kiss her. We were both excited, but Lindsay was nervous too. We were both working nonstop, and our lives already felt out of control. How would a baby fit into that? "Just don't worry," I told her. "We'll make it work."

That summer my dad, Art, and I had many meetings about opening another restaurant. Art liked to joke that I was his best investment, and would ask me when we were going to open up in Vegas. I described my vision for a restaurant that people could use daily. I wanted them to come in for a burger for lunch on Wednesday and then come back on Saturday night and have a full gastronomical experience with a steak and a bottle of Bordeaux. Art got on board right away. "Recette is your laboratory," he told me. "But this has to be a business. It has to make money."

As things got more serious and we started meeting with attorneys and looking at real estate, we realized that we needed a very significant amount of money for a big project like this. Art helped me look for investors and opened up a whole new world for me, sharpening my financial wits along the way. He asked questions I never would have thought of, like how the second restaurant would affect Recette. While I was focused on details like how many seats we could fill, Art taught me to think globally. He also introduced me to people who were instrumental in getting this project off the ground. Whenever we met at the Regency Hotel or for lunch at Sea Grill in Rockefeller Center, dozens of people would come up to Art to say hello. He knew everyone, and after he introduced me I'd go back to the office at Recette, Google them, and find out they ran hedge funds or publicly held companies.

The rest of Lindsay's pregnancy flew by in the blink of an eye. At least, that's how it felt for me. I'm sure it felt a lot longer to her as she worked around the clock at Recette and at home, setting up the nursery and planning for the baby almost completely alone. I was too consumed with work to really notice. Business was booming at Recette, and soon awards started tumbling in. That December, *Forbes* included me as one of its "30 Under 30," an annual list of movers and shakers in the food and wine business who were under thirty years of age.

As I stood in the room with the other honorees, a group of incredibly talented people, it hit me for the first time that my career was truly taking off. Eight years earlier I was just another junkie shooting heroin in a filthy alley behind an abandoned building, and now *Forbes* magazine was recognizing my work. Thank God my desire to use was long gone, but the addictive behavior was still there. Now I was addicted to work, success, and getting the next creative high.

About a month later my mom asked me to meet her for breakfast at the Bus Stop Café, a hole in the wall near Recette. I had been so consumed with work that I had barely spoken to my mother in weeks. The further I got from the center I'd reached in treatment the more I felt old resentments toward my mother creeping in again. It was easier to just shut her out of my life or make backhanded comments under my breath than to actually work on our relationship, but she had requested this meeting, so I agreed to see her.

I woke up that morning feeling anxious, like something wasn't right. I sat down across from my mother at the cafe and listened as she told me how disconnected she felt from me and how sad this made her, but I could barely concentrate. My mind wasn't there. I was thinking about Recette, the second restaurant, and the impending birth of our first child.

In the middle of our breakfast my phone rang. It was my dad, and as soon as I heard his voice I knew something was wrong. He had been trying to reach my mother, who wasn't answering her phone. It was Grandpa Laz. He'd been having chest pains and had been rushed to the hospital. My mom hurried off to be with my dad, and I went to Lindsay at Recette. Despite my years away from the family, Laz and I were still close, and I'd never forgotten the letters he wrote to me in jail when almost everyone else had forsaken me.

I distracted myself by drowning myself in business. At one time drugs had been my only escape from my feelings, but now I had work, and I stormed around the restaurant demanding to know why we were going through so much dish soap and why the waitstaff kept breaking so many glasses. A few hours later we went to my parents' rented studio apartment and listened to my father talking on the phone to his brother, telling him that Laz didn't want to be resuscitated. Before I knew it my grandfather was gone. Sitting on my parents' couch, I started to cry. It was the first time I had shed a tear in years, and the first time Lindsay had ever seen me cry, but she held me as I cried in her arms.

My entire family flew down to Florida the next day for the funeral, but Lindsay was too far along in her pregnancy to fly and there was no way I was going to leave her. I felt awful and wrote a letter that my sister read at Laz's funeral. This wasn't the first time I'd tasted death, but Laz's passing hit me much harder than any other loss I'd experienced. When I was using, I'd fallen out enough times to have an idea of what it must be like to die. Addicts live with thoughts of their own mortality every day. But this was different. I was about to become a father, and life itself held new meaning to me. I didn't want to accept Laz's death. I didn't want to accept the fact that people do, in fact, just die. My uncle Bruce's death and my parents' health issues had scared me in the past, but nothing had scared me quite like this.

When my parents returned to New York after the funeral, my mom came to my apartment and tried to continue the conversation we'd started at the Bus Stop Café. By then I was so wound up with anxiety about work, about the baby on the way, and about Laz's death that I exploded on her. "I think you're shallow, manipulative, and selfish," I told her, holding nothing back. "You may be the most giving person in the world, but it's all about you, and I can't stand it!"

The funny thing was, I didn't really believe those things in the moment; I was merely saying the things I had thought about her when I was a kid. But somehow saying them out loud was incredibly liberating. My mother just listened, and then she hugged me and told me that she was willing to change. And suddenly all the old feelings and resentments melted away and I was able to see my mother for who she really is—an incredibly loving and giving woman who is ultimately human. It struck me that the only thing my mother has ever done to me is love me more than anyone or anything else in the world. She would cut off her arm for me if I asked, and as my childish resentments melted away I realized how much I really do love her.

Just a few days later it was a freezing cold and snowy night when Lindsay and I hailed a cab to go to the Langone Medical Center. She was in labor. Once we checked in and the doctor told us that we probably had several more hours before the baby appeared, I switched into work mode, answering texts and returning calls. Back in the grips of addiction, I was oblivious as Lindsay labored away in the bed next to me. I could only think about work.

Three hours later I got a call from my publicist. "The James Beard Awards are nominating you in two categories," she told me. "Outstanding Restaurant and Rising Star Chef." I hung up the phone in shock. The James Beard Awards are like the Oscars of the culinary world, and they normally go to much older, more established chefs. As Lindsay's labor progressed I couldn't stop thinking about this latest accolade and what it would mean for my career.

I wish I had been there for Lindsay. That day should have been about her hard work, her accomplishment, and the miracle of life we created together. But I couldn't take my eyes off the fucking prize. Every award, every honor, every compliment from a diner, they were all just another version of the same old high, and I was still nothing more than a fucking junkie.

Eddie Harris Schenker was born at 3:49 P.M., and for just a moment the noise quieted as I held him, taking in his small, blue eyes that were wide open and alert. I stood bewildered by my latest creation, swaddled in a blue-and-white-striped hospital blanket. Would we connect as father and son? What would his life be like? Would he be happy and carefree or tormented by some unseen demon like I was? Of course I was worried about what path he would take and whether I would be able to make room in my life and in my heart for this tiny, defenseless human.

As Eddie cried out for his first meal and I handed him to Lindsay I realized that I wanted to be there for him in a way I'd never been there for anyone else. Addicts generally don't do empathy, but I finally knew what it meant to care about someone else more than I cared about myself. For just a moment I felt like there was nothing left to push for or win. Hadn't I just been handed all I could ever ask for?

But for me old habits die hard, and as soon as we brought Eddie home I jumped back into work with the same vengeance as before. Now, while Lindsay stayed at home breast-feeding, changing diapers, and staying up half the night caring for a newborn, I was pounding the pavement with Art looking for a space for the second restaurant, meeting with restaurateurs, and cooking for private parties while working late into the night at Recette. Instead of greeting the day by kissing Eddie and Lindsay in the morning, I'd grab my BlackBerry and disappear into the other room. All I could think about was growing the business.

In the midst of all this my father noticed a strange mole on my mother's backside that turned out to be melanoma. She bravely faced surgery yet again, even though she was still undergoing chemo for the breast cancer. The health issues just kept coming, making me feel even more like my life was snowballing completely out of control. I was a nervous wreck as I pushed in every aspect of my life with all my might and every day waited for the phone to ring with news of some new health crisis.

Six months passed like this before I returned to Florida with Lindsay and Eddie to visit Laz's grave. The day was clear and hot, and as I stared down at the marble headstone bearing his name I thought about happier times in the past when Laz had come to stay with Joee and me when our parents went away. He had always been such a present, patient, loving grandfather. He would have loved Eddie, his thirteenth great-grandchild.

Lindsay, Eddie, and I got back in the car and drove away. After a minute I turned to look at Eddie, who was already half asleep in his car seat. Then I turned to Lindsay. "Let's love each other like Laz and Rosie," she said sweetly. Her words were beautiful, but I didn't think I was capable of living up to them.

CHAPTER SIXTEEN

Au Jus

Au jus: A dish of roasted meat served with its own cooking juices.

When the call came in asking me to appear on *Iron Chef America*, I was incredibly psyched. I'd always loved cooking competition shows like *Iron Chef Japan*, which I watched obsessively as a kid. On *Iron Chef*, I'd be competing against one of four Iron Chefs to make the best five dishes in one hour based on one secret ingredient that wouldn't be revealed until the day of the taping. This meant that I could practice and prepare all I wanted, but I wouldn't know what ingredient needed to be featured until it was showtime.

I dove into the preparations. The first step was to choose two sous chefs to work with me. Right away I knew I wanted Christina Lee so she could help with all the pastry. Jeff Haskell, my former boss at City Cellar, was now in New York working as the executive chef at City Winery. Back when we worked together, Jeff always said, "One day you're going to be on *Iron Chef*," and I told him, "When I am, I'm taking you with me." It felt good to be able to keep my word.

Christina, Jeff, and I began preparing for the battle day

after day, night after night. Of course, I didn't know what the secret ingredient would be, but that didn't stop us. I wrote out four different tasting menus leaving the main ingredient blank so we could fill it in at the last minute with the secret ingredient. Some of these menus worked better with a protein, some with a fruit or vegetable, and others with a grain. I wanted to do five dishes that showed completely different techniques rather than five different versions of the same dish. Each dish would have to show off the secret ingredient in a unique way. For four weeks leading up to the taping, I closed Recette on Sunday evenings so we could practice.

We did three full dry runs to prepare for the battle and spent a lot of time in between watching old episodes of *Iron Chef* and analyzing what gave certain chefs an edge and what the judges looked for. It was clear that creativity, technique, and plating were not enough. In order to win, the food had to taste good; that's what the judges ultimately cared about. I went back and tweaked our menus to make sure they were impressive on a technique level while also tasting as good as possible.

I was a nervous wreck for days leading up to the filming. As Lindsay slept beside me I tossed and turned, ruminating over the menus and wondering if they could possibly be good enough for us to win. "What, are you meeting Art in the morning?" Lindsay asked, reminding me of those sleepless nights before that first meeting with Art, which now felt so long ago. It seemed like there was always something for me to obsessively worry and fret about.

On the day of the filming the Food Network sent a car for me at 5:00 A.M. I was long awake, pacing outside my apartment building, when the car came. The studio, just a few blocks from Recette in Chelsea Market, was much smaller than it looked on TV; it was filled with dozens of crew members, cameras were positioned at every angle, and spotlights covered the ceiling. As I took it all in my eyes fixed on two identical kitchen sets, one for each contestant, with range tops, convection ovens, food processors, blenders, refrigerators, shitloads of kitchenware, and just about every type of food and ingredient imaginable.

My opponent was Geoffrey Zakarian, an older and much more experienced chef. I was definitely intimidated. Zakarian has been around the New York culinary world forever and is a master technician. When we came face-to-face while picking out our plates, he nodded at me and said, "Hi, Chef." It was surreal seeing him in person after watching him so many times on TV. "Hi, Chef," I said, nodding back. But now I was even more intimidated by how calm and well manicured he was. I was a big sweaty mess in comparison.

Soon after we began filming the host lifted the cover on the secret ingredient to reveal . . . plantains. Great. I had exactly one hour to create five courses around an ingredient I didn't like to cook with or even eat. But there wasn't a moment to mourn the secret ingredient. Christina, Jeff, and I did a brief huddle, quickly coming up with a game plan, but we already knew the gist of what we wanted to make. Now we just had to fill in the blanks with plantains. I knew we had to do five completely different things with the plantains, so we made pasta out of it for the first course (Plantain Cannelloni Stuffed with Sweet Shrimp), a terrine for the next (Ripe Plantain Terrine with Jalapeño, Caviar, and Bacon), a play on mashed potatoes for another (Plantain-Crusted Grouper, Plantain Mash, Lobster, and Lobster Emulsion), a takeoff on crème brûlée (Duck Breast with Speck Plantain Brûlée and Plantain Chips), and a sweet mousse for dessert (Sweet Plantain Mousse with Pineapple and Coconut Sorbet).

One after another, the three of us just knocked the dishes out. We didn't stop for a moment—not to check out Zakarian and his crew and not even to check in with each other. I trusted my team and knew that I had to take off the training wheels and let them roll. It was crazy, nonstop fun, and I was running around like a madman, at one point running so fast that a whole grouper slid right out of my hands. But I loved every minute of it. When it was all over and the host announced my name as the winner, I couldn't believe it. I was thrilled to be able to add *"Iron Chef* winner" to my accomplishments.

Soon after filming *Iron Chef,* I flew down to Florida to meet with my dad, and as we drove around one day he said, "Something's not right. My PSA levels are up." My dad has always been a worrier, and I blew him off. "You probably just drank too much coffee before the test or something," I said. But my dad was right. We found out soon after that he had prostate cancer. Coming so soon on the heels of my mother's breast cancer and melanoma, I just couldn't believe it. What was next?

Things kept up at a rapid pace. I was invited to cook at the James Beard House, which is a huge honor for any chef. Foodies from around the city bought tickets to watch me cook in a kitchen that had been used by every notable chef in the world. As I began to prep the food with my team I thought about the fact that I was cooking on the same stove my mentors had used and washing my hands in the same sink as the very chefs who had helped mold my style and shape my career had done. We were cooking for a hundred people who had been invited to walk through the kitchen as we were working. It was an amazing and surreal experience. These diners had eaten food prepared by the world's best chefs, so I knew mine had to be good.

I pulled from the Recette arsenal, coming up with dishes that were salty and acidic and demonstrating a good amount of technique, but not to the point where the food was too artistic or intimidating to eat. We served a little hors d'oeuvre of beef carpaccio wrapped around burrata cheese with tomato jam, a classic flavor combination that used a nontraditional technique. Next were classic French gougères stuffed with a smooth, silky puree of wild mushrooms and Parmesan cheese. We made croquets with good Spanish ham that we folded into béchamel sauce and then breaded, fried, and topped with a salty white anchovy that made the whole thing sing. I reached into my passion for Japanese simplicity and came up with a scallop crudo using amazingly fresh Maine sea scallops. We shucked them out still pulsating, sliced them paper-thin, and served them with just a touch of lemon and olive oil. On top we put a beautiful, sweet sea urchin, one of my favorite ingredients, and a piece of heirloom tomato. I wanted to show technique with a foie gras terrine, which looked like a mosaic when we sliced it. Then we pickled chanterelle mushrooms to make them really acidic and paired them with fatty pork belly and a sweet corn pudding to hit all the flavor profiles. We took delicate, flaky halibut and served it with delicious, thick, creamy mushrooms and lots of caviar. Finally, we served pork three ways: in a fried terrine made from the pork shoulder; a slow roasted, carved loin; and a seared belly that we had braised and pressed.

My team and I set up an assembly line in the kitchen and prepared dish after dish. After we walked through the dining room and answered questions, everyone applauded us. "I couldn't do any of this without my team," I said, and we all felt incredibly proud of pulling off this high-stakes culinary rite of passage.

Meanwhile, I kept single-mindedly pursuing the goal of opening a second restaurant. Through Art, I met another investor named Leon Wagner, whom Art called "the Governor of New York." Indeed, he seemed to know everyone. At our first meeting we sat down to lunch, and I ordered a salad. Lindsay had been on my back about my out-of-control eating habits, and even I had to admit that I needed to lose weight.

"Why are you ordering a salad?" Leon asked me. "Are you on a diet?"

"Not exactly," I told him. "But my wife read me the riot act a couple of weeks ago. We have a one-year-old son, and I want to be around to see him grow up."

Leon paused for a moment. "I want to introduce you to Dr. Stephen Gullo," he told me. "He's one the world's top diet doctors. I'll set it all up. It'll be my treat. This is how we'll christen our partnership."

A few days later Lindsay and I went to Dr. Gullo's office on the Upper East Side feeling antsy and not knowing what to expect. This guy treated celebrities and Academy Award winners; what was he going to say to a mildly obese chef and former junkie like me? Dr. Gullo walked in, and we talked for maybe five minutes before he laid it on the line. "Jesse, you're type A," he told me. "Moderation is not part of your vocabulary." Lindsay and I looked at each other and burst out laughing. This was perhaps the greatest understatement we'd ever heard.

Over the next two hours I told Dr. Gullo everything—when, where, what, and how much I ate, along with the details of my background and history of addiction. He was the only person who knew all this other than my immediate friends and family. Even my closest coworkers, my pastry chef and sous chef didn't know about my past. They knew I didn't drink and probably assumed that I had issues with addiction, but they didn't ask and I didn't tell. Once I was done, Dr. Gullo said, "The sugar in simple carbohydrates can trigger a response in the brain similar to that of cocaine," and I knew in that moment that this guy had me pegged.

I eagerly listened as Dr. Gullo laid out a plan for me. "There are certain things about you that we're not going to change," he said. "You're a chef. You're going to eat late. You have an appetite for life." Instead of changing me or even my habits, Dr. Gullo changed which foods I ate. "Think substitution, not deprivation," he said, writing up a schedule for the week. "If you follow this plan to the letter, I guarantee you'll be down nine pounds in a week."

A week later I was down nine pounds, just as he predicted. Once I saw the results, I put the blinders on and barreled forward, diving into weight loss with my typical determination. This type of singular focus on pursuing a goal is celebrated in our culture, and it certainly helped me achieve my goals, but it also served as a distraction from the issues that lay dormant underneath. The same obsessiveness that drove me to use drugs, to work around the clock, and even to gain weight in the first place now pushed me to lose sixty pounds in mere months. The weight loss was great for my physical health and my appearance, but as the weight came off so did my buffer. My fat had protected me just as drugs and later meetings and spirituality had, and without my weight or my armor, I was left naked and vulnerable. I needed another safe harbor, and I'd soon find it.

A few months before Eddie turned two, Lindsay and I took him up to New Paltz for my cousin Jack's bar mitzvah. My New Paltz family had grown by leaps and bounds—my cousins now had kids of their own, and I loved being back in the fold of that open, loving, chaotic family. At the bar mitzvah they played a video of Jack with his two older siblings, and I caught Lindsay looking at me with those green eyes. I knew what that meant. She wanted another baby, and I had to admit that I did too.

At that bar mitzvah I saw the generations passing before my eyes. The tradition is for the oldest male in the family to say a prayer over the challah, and since Grandpa Laz and Uncle Bruce were both gone, this honor fell to my dad. He was horrified and kept asking me, "Can you believe I've got to cut the fucking challah?" Things were moving too quickly for all of us.

Before long Lindsay and I were expecting our second child. I had no idea how we'd fit another baby into our daily lives, but I didn't stop to think about that. I feared that if I paused for one second to think about anything, it would all tumble around me. The only answer was to keep going, pushing, and striving forward. Nothing would get in the way of me opening a second restaurant and continuing to grow my business and my family.

A couple of months later Lindsay, Eddie, Joee, and I were on our way back to New York from Florida. It was a quiet, uneventful flight, and I sat reading an article in a medical magazine that had been left in the seat pocket in front of me about deep vein thrombosis. Suddenly a surge of energy ran through my entire body, like a wave that went from the top of my head to the tips of my toes. I started fidgeting with my fingers and tapping my feet like I always did as a kid. I couldn't sit still and kept shifting in my seat. My heart was racing, and beads of perspiration formed on my brow.

Deep vein thrombosis. I couldn't get those words out of my head. By the time we got from the airport to our apartment in the West Village, I was dialed in. I immediately sat down at the computer and scoured the Internet for anything I could find on the blood clots that form in a vein deep in the body, nervously reading about how they can travel through the bloodstream and cause a pulmonary embolism. In my rational mind, I knew that I didn't have deep vein thrombosis. I didn't have a single risk factor and probably had a better chance of being struck by lightning than developing DVT, but that didn't matter. After putting Eddie to bed that night, I locked myself in the bathroom and examined my calves. Were they warm, red, and swollen? I searched for hard, wormlike veins, a telltale sign of DVT, and then I made a checklist and ran through every symptom. Lindsay walked in to find me checking the pulse in my left foot. She must've thought I was out of my mind.

My obsession with DVT lasted for days—through meetings with staff, catering events, business meetings, and time with my family. After a week of nonstop ruminating, I moved on to another condition. Quickly it got so bad that Lindsay started keeping a log of my many imagined illnesses. My testicular discomfort had to be cancer. I stayed up all night reading about it and came up with a plan to harvest my sperm in case we wanted to have more kids. One night I went to a colleague's restaurant and scratched my throat on a chicken bone. The next day I was convinced the scratch was esophageal cancer. I even went to an ear, nose, and throat doctor and insisted that he perform a laryngoscopy, which revealed, of course, that I was fine.

The downward spiral was fast and hard. The bulging veins in my temple were the result of blood clots. A mole that had been on my back since I was a kid became metastatic melanoma. The connective tissue around my groin turned into swollen glands. Mild headaches were brewing aneurysms. Blurred vision in my right eye, which turned out to be nothing more than a smudge of dirt on my glasses, was the result of a massive brain tumor. In one terrifying three-week span I believed I had contracted gastritis, colon cancer, colitis, and even necrotizing fasciitis, a fucking flesh-eating bacteria.

I morphed into a madman, visiting urgent care so many times that I thought I was going to be issued a lifetime ban. Every test showed that I was fine. But no level of medical evaluation or reassurance helped. I became obsessed with every one of my bodily functions, habitually misinterpreting normal physical sensations. Just reading about a disease or hearing about a sick friend sent me off the deep end of worry and despair. At the same time I became perversely fascinated with medical information, staying up all night reading medical books the same way I once devoured cookbooks.

For years I'd lived with the scourge of addiction. I hid in bushes, slept on cardboard boxes, OD'd, and dodged bullets, and I survived it all. Now I was plagued with a raw, carnal fear of illness. My body and mind had healed from the savagery of my first twenty-one years, but the scars underneath had caused me to recoil. On the streets and in jail my physical body felt taut enough to withstand the hardest blows, but all along I was a paper tiger. Bruce Lee said, "The stiffest tree is most easily cracked, while the bamboo or willow survives by bending with the wind." I'd grown so rigid in my lack of acceptance that I couldn't unfurl my fingers long enough to hold my child and embrace my wife. I felt broken, snapped in half like an old tree.

In the back of my head, always, was the knowledge that getting high would cure these feelings. Every day I lived on the edge, knowing that I was one pill away from losing everything I had achieved. Finally my internist told me that I didn't need another medical test. "I'm going to recommend that you speak to a psychologist," he told me. "And I'm going to write you a prescription for Celexa." In less than ten years I'd gone from a homeless junkie to a successful workaholic. But nothing had changed. I had just substituted one drug for another.

Whether or not to take the Celexa was a big decision. Since getting clean, I hadn't taken one sip of beer or any pill stronger than Tylenol. I worried that the Celexa would lead to a stronger pill, and then a stronger one, and then an even stronger one after that. But I was even more afraid of continuing on the path I was already on. I started taking the Celexa, and it helped take the edge off, giving me room to breathe. Slowly the anxiety lessened, and I was able to do the work I needed to do to become whole again.

Thank God Lindsay stepped in too. "You lost your center," she told me. "You need another anchor." With her support, I went back to AA, first one meeting a week, then two, three, and sometimes more. I began intensive weekly phone sessions with Larry Kreisberg, the therapist I'd first seen as a teenager, and I started seeing a cognitive behavioral therapist once a week to help work on my hypochondriasis.

After one meeting I approached an older man who had spoken. "I'm coming up on nine years of sobriety," I told him, shaking slightly as I held my coffee cup, "and I've lost my way." He agreed to be my sponsor, and I renewed my commitment to working the steps, connecting to other addicts, and being of service. I began to chair a meeting every other week and found time in the midst of the chaos for reflection.

In meetings and in therapy with Larry I realized that I had first started to go off course when I moved to New York and took my will back. In treatment I had found a way to live in a middle-ground, temperate zone, but as I got excited about the food at Ramsay and then about starting my own business, I was gradually pulled away from that middle. And then it became far too easy for me to lose myself in the extremes of work, eating, success, and anxiety.

As I worked on myself my life continued to move forward at a frenetic pace. I tried to refocus on acceptance as I continued hunting for a space for a second restaurant, homing in on a four-block radius in the Flatiron District that had heavy foot traffic and a good mix of restaurants, shops, and businesses. Every time a potential space fell through, I reminded myself that it wasn't meant to be. But as we were outbid on spaces over and over, my anxiety crept back up. I couldn't accept the possibility of failure.

Luckily, we got some relief where I least expected it. Eddie's former babysitter worked part-time at Allison 18, a restaurant in the Flatiron District with a straightforward, New American, bistro-style menu. One afternoon Lindsay and I stopped in with Eddie to check out the place, and I couldn't believe my eyes. The restaurant was a dream—a huge, wood-paneled dining room with enough space to fit 150 people plus a private dining room downstairs with a bar that could seat another 75. The dining room had a clean, casual vibe with purple banquettes lining the walls and wallpaper covered with New York City street scenes. It was as if Allison 18 had been custom-made to fit my vision.

I didn't think about it much at the time, but when I heard that Allison 18 was going under and the landlord was taking bids, I knew this was the one, and I was nervous. So many potential deals had already slipped through my fingers. There was already a bid on the space, and I couldn't risk losing it. So I spoke to my investors, and we fired back with a much higher bid. The landlord hesitated, so we bid even higher. I had to get this done. And we did. The landlord accepted our bid, and the entire restaurant—from the china to the walk-in and the custom ovens and ventilation system—would be mine.

Lindsay was due with our second child any day as we began the back-and-forth with attorneys to work out the minutiae of the lease—the rent abatement, liquor license, stipulations, guarantors, and indemnification. Recette was still happening, but it wasn't new anymore, so I continued to put myself out there and accept catering gigs and media appearances whenever I could.

On October 9, 2013, Lindsay gave birth to our daughter, Liv Rose. This time I was present in the delivery room both physically and mentally, but it was Lindsay's turn to be distracted. She was on her iPad responding to emails right up until the moment it was time to start pushing, lying in the hospital bed processing payroll and emailing back and forth with our publicist. "Lindsay, you have to get off the iPad. The baby's coming," the doctor reminded her. I had taken my wife and created a monster, but I'd never been prouder of her.

It was exciting for both our family and our restaurant "family" to be expanding at the same time, and I worked hard to live in the moment and not let that excitement pull me too far to the extremes. In December we signed the lease for my second restaurant, The Gander. It felt right, but the stakes were higher than ever. I was responsible for more money and people than ever before. Recette had only twenty-five employees, but I needed to hire a hundred people to run The Gander. Plus, there was more money on the line and more investors to satisfy. And as with Recette, I felt a deep need to touch every nut and bolt of this restaurant and make sure that every detail was perfect.

The first thing I did was put together my team—Christina Lee as pastry chef, Christina Han as director of culinary development, Ed stepping up to a corporate chef role, and James, whom I worked with at Gordon Ramsay, as my chef de cuisine. Christina Han, James, and I started working on the menu. I was inspired by a documentary about how renowned Spanish chef Ferran Adrià came up with new seasonal menus at his restaurant El Bulli by testing each recipe and grading it on a star system. One star meant it was weak, two stars meant it needed work, three stars meant it was almost there, and four stars meant it was perfect. I took on this system, and we worked around the clock to create a menu of three- and four-star dishes.

The food at The Gander was different from what I was used to cooking, and I was determined to use great technique while creating dishes that were familiar yet memorable. This was no easy task. We spent weeks just talking about the concept and coming up with ideas. I thought about the foods I loved to order in restaurants and how I could put my own spin on them here. I love Caesar salads and wedge salads, for instance, so I had the idea to combine them into a wedge salad with Caesar dressing. But I couldn't stop there. I had to make it my own, and we played around with a million variations—overcompensating with more dressing on the outside and less on the inside, and later squirting dressing in between each layer of lettuce leaves so that every bite was perfectly balanced, acidic, and crunchy. The breadcrumbs we put on top alone took days of experimenting as we tried toasting them, cooking them in olive oil, and tossing them in butter.

I wanted all of the food at The Gander to be approachable. Brisket is familiar and delicious, and we started playing around with making brisket croquettes as a salty fried snack. We braised the brisket with wine and herbs and then shredded it, reduced the braising liquid, and folded the meat back in. Once it set, we rolled the meat into cylinders, cut the cylinders into inch-long pieces, breaded them with flour and breadcrumbs, and fried them. They were just okay. The dish needed a twist.

A few days later my general manager randomly told me about a dream he had about a patty melt. That was all the inspiration I needed. I ran into the kitchen and tried the croquettes again, this time adding caraway and rye flour, mozzarella cheese, and caramelized onions. It was much better, maybe three stars. Over time we started breading the croquettes in potato starch, and they morphed into a combination of a tater tot and a croquette with the familiar flavors of a patty melt. Finally I was satisfied.

The restaurant already had a rotisserie, and I was determined to use it for more than just cooking chicken. I wondered what would happen if we used it to treat vegetables like proteins. I took a whole head of cauliflower and marinated it overnight in a mixture of olive oil, garlic, anchovy paste, lemon, and herbs, taking inspiration from the classic Italian version. Then I skewered it and cooked it in the rotisserie. It came out even better than I expected, with bold flavors and varying textures, the outside pieces being crunchier and the inside gradually growing softer.

A few weeks before The Gander opened I hosted a preview of the new menu for the media right in the middle of the restaurant during construction. Journalists came from *Travel + Leisure, Bon Appétit, Time* magazine, Zagat, the *Wall Street Journal,* the New York *Daily News,* and Bloomberg Media, and we served the wedge Caesar salad, brisket croquettes, rotisserie cauliflower, and a pasta dish with a whole suckling pig that we cooked in the rotisserie and then shredded. It was our first time cooking for other people in the new kitchen, and I was my regular manic self, tasting everything twenty-five times, reseasoning every dish, and meticulously inspecting everything that came out of the kitchen. In between courses I went out to the dining room and talked to the journalists, answering their questions about The Gander's concept and inspiration.

Too many restaurants are pretentious and stuffy, and when I saw those journalists, who were technically working, eating and drinking and laughing unself-consciously, I knew that my dream would be realized. The Gander would serve as a meeting place for people who wanted to shake off their cares and worries, eat good food, and have fun.

On the cab ride home late that night Lindsay rested her head on my chest and I thought about how blessed I was. Despite all the bad choices I'd made in life, I had a beautiful family and a good relationship with my extremely generous and forgiving parents and sister. Ten years before, they didn't know if I was alive or dead, and now we enjoyed a closer relationship than most men my age have with their families. My parents aren't only an essential part of my business, but also wonderful and involved grandparents to Eddie and Liv. My sister, Joee, and I are closer than ever. We have fun together, and she's an amazing aunt who spends as much time as possible with my kids. It struck me that despite how much my addiction had hurt my family, it also helped all of us get out of the cycle of codependency and develop stronger, healthier relationships.

Thinking back to the moment I hit bottom and called my parents from that seedy hotel room, I was in awe of the way they cut me off at the knees right when I needed it. As a parent, I could now plainly feel how painful it must have been for them to do that, and I was so grateful that they did. I owed my parents everything, I realized. They gave me a great life, and when I ruined it they did the most difficult thing a parent can do, ultimately giving me a new one.

Now I had reached a level of personal and professional success I couldn't have imagined when I was smoking crack on the streets of Florida, and that wouldn't have been possible if my parents hadn't found the strength to let me go. Sure, I still struggled with the day-to-day anxieties of running a business and raising a family, but I was a completely different person than the one I'd been ten years before. I was a productive member of society and, most important to me, I lived with integrity. This was the serenity I had been searching for my whole life, and I vowed not to let it slip through my fingers yet again.

When we got home, I paused in front of my daughter's crib and watched her sleeping, transfixed by her beautiful little face. Her rhythmic breathing always brought momentary peace to my hectic universe. After a while I moved to Eddie's room. The bed was empty, but the mattress, which he'd pushed up against the wall, was occupied, with his feet where his head should have been and a pacifier resting next to his open mouth. I knelt down next to his mattress and listened to his deep and relaxed breathing, each inhale and exhale suggesting a child's clear conscience and carefree existence. Children are the epitome of living in the moment, and that is still the ultimate goal for me—to keep my balance and acceptance so that I can live in the moment with them.

During one of our recent phone sessions my therapist Larry started talking about my cooking. I was surprised; this was one topic we normally didn't cover. "When you're making a dish, what happens if you leave out an ingredient?" he asked me.

"The whole thing falls apart," I answered automatically.

"Exactly," Larry said, as if I had just hit on something brilliant. "Your life is a recipe," he continued. "It's made of therapy, meetings, service, work, and family, and you need every ingredient to make it work."

Of course I still slip sometimes. I take on too much and miss a meeting and my anxiety level starts to rise, or I dive into work in the morning before embracing my family and become depressed and filled with remorse. I may not be healed, but I am whole. And with the same dogged persistence that I use to craft each dish in my kitchen, I will keep working until I perfect the recipe of my life.

Acknowledgments

Mom & Dad: You have been so selfless and giving, and without you this life wouldn't be possible. You've had to make really hard decisions and put yourselves aside to do the right thing for me and save my life. You have loved me and guided me unconditionally; your love has no end. I owe you everything and am forever grateful to have the most wonderful, loving, and nurturing parents who molded me into the man and father I am today.

Lindsay Schenker, my wife, my best friend, my partner, and the mother of my children: You never let me down and you continue to be my biggest strength in navigating this world. There is no one I'd rather be experiencing all these ever-changing emotions with than you. Thank you.

Joee Schenker, my beautiful older sister: Over the years, you've always supported me no matter what. You're the best sister and aunt anyone could ask for. I love you for eternity.

Eddie & Liv: I love you both more than life itself. You

keep me so humble and teach me every day. Being with you is the only thing that brings time to a halt. I've learned how to be in the moment because of you.

Everyone in my life whom I've crossed paths with—good and bad—you know who you are: All the experiences we've had together led me to the life I know today. To all of my family, friends, and coworkers: Thank you for making my life so rich. And to all of you who weren't so positive: I appreciate you for giving me the courage, strength, and patience to survive on the ugly side of this world. Together as a whole, I feel blessed for everyone and everything I've lived through.

Thank you to David Nayor, Celeste Fine, Mark Chait, and the whole crew at HarperCollins, Sterling Lord Literistic, and Dey Street Books for making this project come to life. A special thanks to Jodi Lipper for helping me write this thing and turn my stream-of-conscious thoughts into this book, *All or Nothing*.

Pearl Jam: You've been there the WHOLE way.

Jesse Schenker is executive chef and owner of Recette, which he opened with his wife, Lindsay, in New York's Greenwich Village in 2010. The James Beard Rising Star Semifinalist was included in Zagat's "30 Hottest Chefs Under 30" and *Forbes* magazine's "30 Under 30." He was named Best New Chef by *New York* magazine and beat Chef Geoffrey Zakarian in an *Iron Chef America* battle. His new restaurant, The Gander, opened in April 2014. He lives in New York City.